Let's Talk

Speaking and Listening Activities for Intermediate Students

Leo Jones

Robert Gallo
2342 - John Campbell
Lasalle, Qc. H8N 1C4
Tel:(514)367-3204 Fax:(514)367-3477
E-Mail: robertg@inforoute.net

CAMBRIDGE
UNIVERSITY PRESS

PUBLISHED BY THE PRESS SYNDICATE OF THE UNIVERSITY OF CAMBRIDGE
The Pitt Building, Trumpington Street, Cambridge CB2 1RP, United Kingdom

CAMBRIDGE UNIVERSITY PRESS
The Edinburgh Building, Cambridge CB2 2RU, United Kingdom
40 West 20th Street, New York, NY 10011-4211, USA
10 Stamford Road, Oakleigh, Melbourne 3166, Australia

First published 1996
Second printing 1998

Printed in the United States of America

Typeset in Baskerville Book

Library of Congress Cataloging-in-Publication Data
Jones, Leo, 1943–
Let's Talk! : speaking and listening activities for intermediate
students / Leo Jones.
     p.   cm.
ISBN 0-521-46753-5
1. English language – Textbooks for foreign speakers. 2. English
language – Spoken English – Problems, exercises, etc. 3. Listening –
Problems, exercises, etc.   I. Title.
PE1128.J634   1996
428.3'4–dc20   95-26524
                                        CIP

*A catalogue record for this book is available from
the British Library*

ISBN 0 521 46753 5 Student's Book
ISBN 0 521 46752 7 Teacher's Manual
ISBN 0 521 46754 3 Cassettes

Book design; layout and design services: Adventure House

Illustrators:
Adventure House
Paulette Bogan
David Gothard
Randy Jones
Wally Neibart

Contents

Author's acknowledgments

Many people contributed their hard work, fresh ideas, helpful encouragement, and sound advice to this book.

Thank you to the **reviewers** for their suggestions: Steven Brown, Marin Burch, Steve Cornwell, Alexandre Figueiredo, Ardis Flenniken, Donna Fujimoto, Sally Gearhart, Christa Hansen, Lisa Hori, Suzanne Koons, Christopher Lynch, Jackie Maguire, Christine Salica, Rogerio Sanches, Chuck Sandy, and Aviva Smith.

I would also like to acknowledge the **students** and **teachers** in the following schools and institutes who piloted components of *Let's Talk:* **Boston University,** Boston, Massachusetts, U.S.A.; **Center for English Studies,** New York City, New York, U.S.A.; **Centro Cultural Brasil-Estados Unidos,** Belém, Brazil; **Nagasaki Junior College of Foreign Languages,** Nagasaki, Japan; **Nanzan Junior College,** Nagoya, Japan; **Southern Illinois University,** Niigata, Japan; **University of Pittsburgh,** Pittsburgh, Pennsylvania, U.S.A.; **University of Southern California,** Los Angeles, California, U.S.A.

Thanks to the **editorial** and **production team:** Mary Vaughn guided the whole project from start to finish. Kathy Niemczyk and Stephanie Karras edited the book. Sarah Coleman provided guidance in the early development of the manuscript. Mary Carson provided research assistance. Naomi Ben-Shahar researched the photos. Phyllis Dolgin produced the audio recordings, in conjunction with engineer Steve Day at Dan Kornfeld Recording. Sandra Graham commented on and collated reviews of earlier versions of the manuscript.

Finally, a special thanks to the Cambridge University Press **staff** and **advisors:** Carlos Barbisan, Colin Bethell, Riitta da Costa, Kyoko Fukunaga, Deborah Goldblatt, Jinsook Kim, Carine Mitchell, Sabina Sahni, Helen Sandiford, Kumiko Sekioka, Koen Van Landeghem, and Ellen Zlotnick.

To the student

Let's Talk is about communication. It is about listening to and understanding other people's ideas, and about sharing your ideas with your fellow students.

Be brave! Mistakes are an important part of the learning process, and by reaching for new language you will make progress, even if you sometimes make a mistake. Your partners and teacher will correct the mistakes that prevent you from communicating effectively.

There are 14 units in *Let's Talk*. Every unit includes these activities:

Pair work and Group work   These activities give you a chance to express your ideas and to hear the views of other students in the class. There are many pair and group work exercises in the book so that you can have plenty of speaking practice.

Listening exercises   In real life it is necessary to listen carefully in order to understand new information. The listening exercises in *Let's Talk* are based on authentic dialogues recorded on cassette, and each is accompanied by tasks for you to do as you listen. There are charts to fill in, notes to take, or "matching" exercises, where you decide on the right picture for each dialogue. You can discuss your reaction to the recorded dialogues in the pair or group work activities that follow most listenings.

Readings   Not every unit contains a reading selection, but where there *is* one, the reading will give you new information and ideas for discussion. Each reading is followed by discussion activities so that you can give your opinion about the information presented, or share information on a related topic.

Communication tasks   In each unit there is a communication task for you to do with a partner or group. These tasks give you a chance to practice your English in an informal setting. Sometimes you will be asked to look at photos and decide on a story for the photos. At other times you will be asked to exchange information with a partner or partners. Related communication tasks are on different pages so that you can't read each other's information. The instructions in each unit tell you which task to turn to at the back of the book.

Let's Talk will help you to enjoy using English while also widening your vocabulary and improving your grammatical accuracy. But you've read enough for the moment – now, let's talk!

Activity A **1 Pair work** Where are these people? What are they doing? Describe each scene using the words in the box or your own words.

peaceful/busy
relaxing/stressful
boring/interesting
casual/formal
clean/dirty
crowded/deserted
friendly/unfriendly
quiet/noisy

2 Pair work Which scene do you like best? least? Put the photos in order of preference. Then explain your reasons.

> I like the barbecue scene best because . . .   I don't really like to . . .
> I like . . . least because . . .   I'm not interested in . . .
> I really enjoy going . . .

Activity B **1 Pair work** Choose your favorite color and a color you don't like. Then choose one more color that you like or dislike. Compare with your partner.

red   brown   black   yellow   purple   pink   green   blue   white

2 Pair work Read this chart. Do you and your partner have the personality described for your favorite colors?

WHAT DOES YOUR FAVORITE COLOR SAY ABOUT YOUR PERSONALITY?

BLACK	You are intelligent and love to discuss serious things.
BLUE	You like fresh air and being outdoors, and you like cold weather.
BROWN	You like to be in charge and tell others what to do.
GREEN	You care about the environment and love animals.
PINK	You love to laugh and don't take things too seriously.
PURPLE	You like to be alone and "do your own thing."
RED	You have strong feelings and a quick temper.
WHITE	You love things to be neat and clean, and you always plan ahead.
YELLOW	You are a happy, friendly person, and you love being in the sun.

> You don't like the color black, but you're certainly intelligent, and you enjoy discussing . . .
> We both like the color purple, but we both like to be with people, and we don't like to be alone.

Activity C

1 Pair work You're going to join another pair. But before you join them, try to guess the place they preferred on page 2 and their favorite color.

Name		
Preferred place		
Favorite color		

2 Join another pair Tell them your guesses. What do you think each person's favorite place and color tell you about his or her personality?

> I think your favorite color is probably . . . because . . .
> I think you probably liked the party scene best because . . .
> I think you probably don't like . . . because . . .

Activity D **Communication task** Work with a partner. One of you should look at Task 1 on page C-2, and the other at Task 12 on page C-8. You're going to interview each other about some of your habits and personal qualities.

2 Breaking the ice

Breaking the ice means *"starting a conversation with someone you don't know."*
(Do you have a similar expression in your language? Can you translate it into English?)

Activity A

1 Pair work Look at these pictures. In the United States and Canada, people often start conversations in these situations.
- Would you want to start a conversation in these situations?
  Write YES or NO in each box. Explain your reasons.
- If you answer YES, write a good "icebreaking" remark under the picture.

1. It's the first week of class.

2. You're stuck in an elevator.

3. You see a tourist who needs help.

4. A coworker needs help sending a fax.

2 Listen 📼 Compare your ideas with the recording. Is your "icebreaker" used? (The recording gives just one possible version of each conversation.)

3 Listen again 📼 Read the questions below. Do you hear these icebreakers in the recording? Check (✔) YES or NO. In which conversation do you hear each question? Write the number.

	YES	NO	CONVERSATION #
1. Do you need a hand?			
2. Is this seat taken?			
3. How do you like this class?			
4. Does this happen all the time?			
5. Do you need any help?			
6. Where do you live?			

Activity B

1 Pair work Discuss these questions.
- Do you find it difficult to start conversations? Why or why not?
- Imagine that you want to start a conversation in one of these situations. Can you think of an icebreaker?

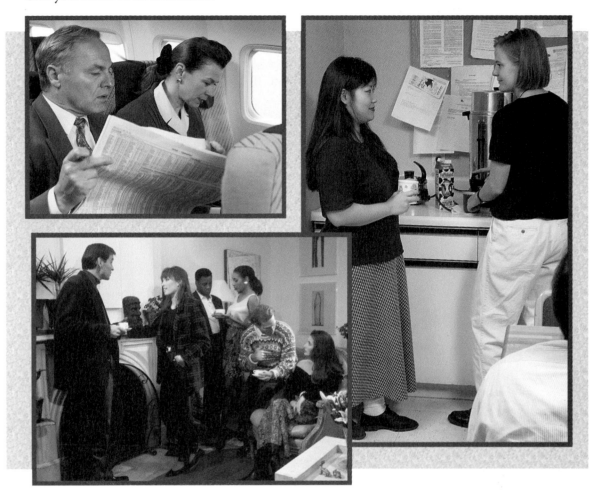

- Think of three other situations where you might want to start a conversation. Write the situation and a possible icebreaker in the chart below.

Situation	Icebreaker

2 Pair work Choose a situation either from the photos above or from the chart you filled out. Act it out, using an icebreaker to start the conversation. Is it successful or unsuccessful?

> Are you going to . . . on vacation?   Haven't we met before?
> What did you think of the meeting?   It's a great party, isn't it?
> Are you new here?

3 Getting to know more about you . . .

1 Read/listen 🔲 First read the article and try to guess the missing words. Then listen and check your answers.

FIRST IMPRESSIONS

According to psychologists, people form first impressions based first on how you look, then on how you _____, and finally on what you say.

Your physical appearance – how you _____ – makes up 55% of a first impression. This includes facial expressions, body language, and eye contact, as well as _____ and general appearance.

The way you sound makes up _____ % of the first impression. This includes how fast or slowly, loudly or softly you _____, and your tone of voice. People listen to your tone of voice and decide whether you sound _____ or unfriendly, interested or bored, and happy or sad. What you say – the actual words you use – counts for only 7% of the message.

People form their first impressions within _____ seconds of meeting you. And first impressions don't change easily.

If someone gets the wrong impression of you, it can take a long time to change his or her mind.

Sometimes it is hard to make sure that you always give a _____ first impression. One problem is that in different parts of the world, the same behavior may give people a different _____. In some countries, looking directly at someone is polite. It shows you are alert and confident. In other countries, looking directly at someone is considered aggressive. It is more polite to look _____. Standing close to someone is considered friendly and supportive in some countries. In others, you are expected to keep your _____.

Giving a good first impression depends on many things. Everyone _____ in different ways, but when you're not sure you're giving a good impression, the best thing to do is ask yourself, "What would *I* think of someone who acted this way?"

2 Pair work Look at this list of things you might do when you meet someone for the first time. Check (✔) the things you usually do. Put an X next to the things you never do.

☐ shake hands
☐ use his/her first name
☐ ask what his/her job is
☐ buy him/her a drink
☐ ask how much he/she earns
☐ look at him/her directly
☐ smile and laugh a lot
☐ bow to him/her

☐ kiss him/her on the cheek
☐ find out what his/her interests are
☐ find out about his/her family
☐ give him/her your business card
☐ touch him/her on the arm
☐ stand very close to him/her
☐ hug him/her when you say good-bye
☐ put your hands in your pockets and lean against the wall

For the items that you never do, can you think of a country where someone would act this way?

3 Join another pair Compare your greeting habits. Is everyone in your group alike? Is anyone different?

1 Listen 🔲 Michael and Amy are being interviewed. First read the questions below. Then listen and write the answers.

1. What are Michael's favorite subjects in school? ....
2. Why does Michael like history? ....
3. What does he want to do when he finishes high school? ....
4. What does he want to do after college? ....

5. What are Amy's favorite subjects in school? ....
6. According to Amy, which language is the most useful? ....
7. Where does Amy want to work? ....
8. Where does she want to live? Why? ....

2 Listen again 🔲 Write five questions the interviewer asks Michael. Then write five things the interviewer says to encourage Amy to say more.

Interview with Michael Questions:	**Interview with Amy** *Encouraging sounds and phrases:*
What's your favorite class?	*Uh-huh.*

3 Join a partner Compare your notes.

1 Pair work Do the questions in the left column or the questions in the right column encourage someone to say something more? Why?

Do you live in an apartment or a house?   *Where do you live?*
Do you like living there?   *How do you like living there?*
Is it because . . . ?   *Why is that?*

2 Work alone Write five questions you could ask someone you have just met.

Examples   *Where are you from originally?*
What kind of music do you like?
What do you think of this weather?

3 Join a partner Form a pair with a different student. Ask your partner questions to find out more about him or her. Then tell the class something you learned about your partner.

4 How do you cook that?

1 Pair work Fill out this chart about your partner's favorite foods. Tell each other why you like the things you do.

What's your favorite?

What's your favorite . . . ?

hot drink

cold drink

main course

appetizer

vegetable

dessert

foreign food

snack

What do you like to cook?

What's your "specialty" (the best thing you cook)?

What's your favorite restaurant?

2 Join another pair Compare your answers. Then discuss these questions.
- What's your least favorite in each category of the chart?
- What foods bring back your best memories?
- Are you someone who "lives to eat" or "eats to live"?

3 Group work Circle the words below that you don't know. Ask your group to explain them. Use a dictionary to look up the words that none of you know. Then add two more items to each list.

Ways of preparing food	peel slice stir beat whip marinate
Ways of cooking	fry deep-fry broil grill bake steam melt roast
Equipment	frying pan skillet roasting pan saucepan pot oven burner steamer

1 Listen 🎧 Three people are describing their favorite dishes. Check (✔) the ingredients in each recipe.

Recipe 1	Recipe 2	Recipe 3
✔ one flounder	☐ chicken pieces	☐ flour
☐ soy sauce	☐ red pepper	☐ salt
☐ garlic	☐ garlic salt	☐ milk
☐ scallions (green onions)	☐ garlic powder	☐ cream
☐ ginger slices	☐ thyme	☐ water
☐ vegetable oil	☐ oregano	☐ eggs
☐ rice	☐ seasoned salt	☐ butter
	☐ beans	☐ cheese
	☐ peanut oil	

375° Fahrenheit = 190° Celsius
1 cup = about 24 centiliters

2 Listen again 🎧 Complete the instructions with the missing words.

Favorite Dishes

① Tony is from _____ .

Steamed flounder with ginger and scallions

1. Marinate the _____ in soy sauce overnight.
2. _____ the fish for three to four minutes.
3. Place scallions and _____ slices on top of the fish and steam for three or four more minutes.
4. Then pour hot _____ over the flounder and serve.

② Wanda is from _____ .

"Mama Pearl's double-seasoned fried chicken"

1. Season the chicken pieces.
2. Then fill a _____ paper _____ halfway with flour and seasoning.
3. Put the chicken pieces inside the bag, close the top, and _____ .
4. Then fry the chicken in a _____ until the pieces are brown.
5. _____ the chicken on a brown paper bag and serve.

③ Trevor is from _____ .

Yorkshire pudding

1. Take one cup of _____ , half a teaspoon of _____ , half a cup of milk, _____ of water, and two eggs.
2. _____ the ingredients together until the mixture is smooth.
3. _____ a quarter of a cup of butter and place it in a pan with the other ingredients.
4. Then bake in the _____ for thirty minutes at _____ degrees. Serve with roast beef.

3 Join a partner Compare your answers. Then discuss these questions.
- Which dish sounds the most delicious?
- What do you think you might *not* like about it?
- Which dish do you think is the easiest to make? Would you consider making it? Which do you think is the hardest to make?

4 Pair work Think of a dish that is popular in your family. Use the vocabulary from Activity A3 to tell your partner the recipe.

5 Join another pair Swap recipes. Which dishes would you like to try?

5 Going out to eat

1 Pair work Imagine that you're sitting together in a restaurant. Read the menu and decide what you want to order from it.

Menu

Appetizers

Shrimp cocktail – fresh shrimp on a bed of chopped lettuce with a tasty seafood sauce
French onion soup – traditional soup topped with French bread and melted cheese
Fresh asparagus – served with melted butter or homemade mayonnaise

Main Dishes

T-bone steak – broiled and served with french fries and steamed vegetable of the day
Spaghetti and meatballs – homemade pasta with meatballs in tomato sauce, served with a green salad
Tempura – fresh seafood and vegetables dipped in egg batter and deep-fried
Fajitas – slices of steak and chicken grilled with green peppers and onions, served with hot flour tortillas
Caesar salad – lettuce topped with a dressing made of anchovies, eggs, and cheese, served with hot French bread
Vegetarian plate – a selection of grilled vegetables served with rice or a baked potato

Desserts

Homemade ice cream: chocolate, vanilla, strawberry, coffee
Banana split – a giant banana with ice cream, nuts, chocolate syrup, and whipped cream
Tropical fruit salad – a generous selection of papaya, mangoes, and pineapple, with a hint of lime
Homemade apple pie – baked in our own kitchen, served with vanilla ice cream or whipped cream

Special today! Two-for-one offer!
Two people ordering exactly the same items from this menu pay for just ONE meal.
(Drinks and tip extra)

What are you going to have?
Would you like . . . ?
. . . sounds good.

I feel like having . . .
I'm going to have . . .
I've changed my mind. I'd like to have . . .

---

2 Join another pair Imagine that you see a couple of friends sitting at another table. Join them and sit together. Explain what you have decided to order.

Now you notice the "two-for-one offer" at the bottom of the menu. Decide whether you want to change your minds about your orders and take advantage of the offer.

Does anyone want to order . . . ?
Why don't we both have . . . ?
Do you feel like . . . ?

Maybe we should have . . .
I'd rather have . . . because . . .

1 Pair work Look at the pictures. What question or statement do you think starts each exchange? Write your guess on the *first* line below each picture.

....

....

....

....

....

....

....

....

....

....

....

....

2 Listen Write the question or statement that actually started each exchange on the *second* line below each picture. Then compare answers with your partner.

Communication task Work in groups of three. Write a menu featuring some typical dishes from different parts of your country. (If the members of your group come from different countries, write a menu for an international restaurant, featuring dishes from each country.) Then one person in your group should look at Task 2 on page C-2, and the other two at Task 13 on page C-8.

6 Families

1 Pair work Discuss these questions.
- Do you know the meaning of these words?

grandmother	daughter	sister	wife	stepmother	niece
mother	granddaughter	sister-in-law	ex-wife	widow	cousin

- What's the masculine equivalent of the words above?
- What words can be combined with *in-law*?
- Look at the family tree below. Explain how James is related to the other people in the chart.

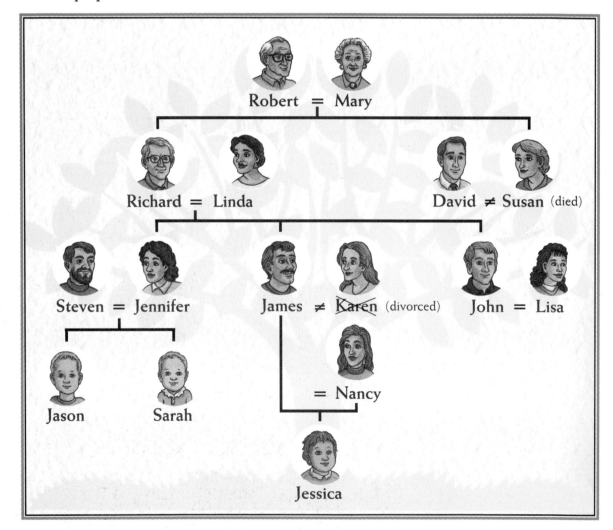

2 Work alone Draw your own family tree.

3 Join a partner Explain "who is who" in your family. Who are your favorite relatives? Why do you like them?

Activity B   **1 Work alone**   Write six words that you associate with the idea of family life.

....

....

....

2 Group work   Compare words with your group. Which words did the other students write? Why did they choose each word? Ask them to explain. Then discuss these questions.
- What are the advantages and disadvantages of living with your family?
- How has family life in your country changed since your parents were your age?

> *One of the nicest things about living at home is . . .*
> *One of the problems of living with your parents is . . .*
> *When my parents were my age, they used to . . .*

Activity C   **Pair work**   Look at these photographs. How are the people in each picture related to each other? Give reasons for your answers.

7 Friends

1 Pair work   The people in the pictures below are friends. Look at the photos and discuss these questions. Decide on a story for each picture.
- What's happening in each picture?
- What happened before the scene shown in each photo?
- What will happen after the scene shown in each photo?

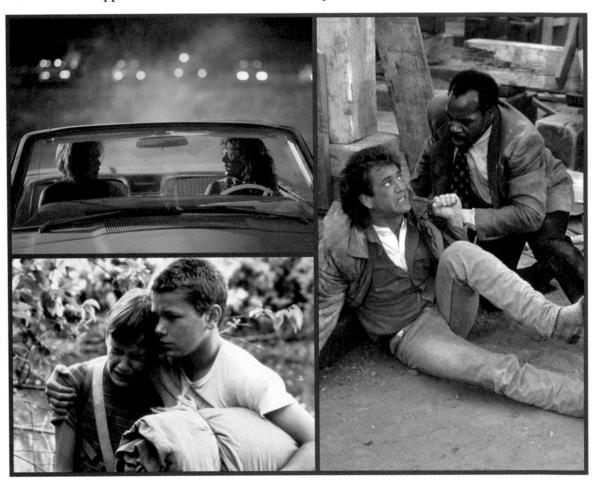

2 Join another pair   Tell your stories to each other.

> My guess is that . . .
> Before this scene happened, . . .
> After this scene, . . . will . . .

1 Listen 🔲 Three people are talking about their friends. Write just one of the reasons they say they get along well with each friend. Write one of the things they do together.

	Why they get along	What they do together
Tom's old friend Jeff		
Tom's new friend Erica		
Lori's old friend Steven		
Lori's new friend Mary		
Phyllis's old friend Dorothy		

2 Group work Compare your notes. Then discuss these questions.
- Are any of the friendships above similar to your own relationships?
- Who is your oldest friend? How did you first meet? Why did you become friends?
- Who is your newest friend? How did you meet and why did you become friends?
- How long do your friendships usually last?
- Why would you stop being friends with someone? Give some reasons.

> I met my oldest/newest friend in . . .
> We get along so well because . . .
> We have/We used to have so much in common because . . .
> I would stop being friends with someone if he/she . . .

3 Listen 🔲 We asked Tom, Lori, and Phyllis this question: "Why are friends important to you?" Take notes on their answers.

Tom	
Lori	
Phyllis	

4 Join a partner Compare your notes. Who do you agree with most: Tom, Lori, or Phyllis?

5 Group work Discuss these questions.

- Look at the list below. Which things would you expect a good friend to do for you? Which things would *you* do for a friend?
- What else do real friends do for each other? Add some items to the list.

take the blame for something you did	travel across the city to see you
write you a letter every week	lend you money
pay for you in a restaurant	let you win a game against him/her
listen to your problems	remember your birthday
phone you every day	give you advice
tell the truth, even if it hurts	send you flowers
keep a secret	not talk behind your back
not hold a grudge	be a friend when times are rough
....	....
....	....

I expect a good friend to . . .
I don't think a friend has to . . .
I would always/never . . . for a friend.
Real friends always/never . . .

Activity C   **Communication task**   Work with a partner. Each of you is going to choose someone you would like to be friends with. Their pictures are below.

Now one of you should look at Task 3 on page C-3, and the other at Task 14 on page C-9.

Review puzzles

Puzzle A   The words in this puzzle are from Lessons 1–3. Read the sentences below. Then complete the puzzle with the missing words.

1. When you want to start a conversation with a stranger, it's always good to use an .... .
2. If you like to be alone and "do your own thing," you probably like the color .... .
3. .... appearance makes up 55% of a first impression.
4. .... that you want to start a conversation with someone. What would you say?
5. *Can I give you a* .... *?* is another way of saying *Do you need some help?*
6. People notice each other's .... language as well as the words they say to each other.

7. Looking directly at someone is called .... contact.
8. The way you .... makes up 38% of a first impression.
9. You have to be .... and speak softly in a library.
10. It was a .... dinner party. Guests were dressed in their best clothes.

11. What is your favorite .... in school?
12. When you meet someone for the first time, do you usually use his or her first .... ?
13. He gets angry very easily. He has a .... temper.
14. *How do you* .... *this class?* is a good icebreaker.

15. (down) A good friend would never talk about you ....

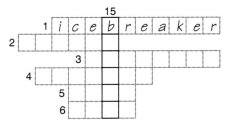
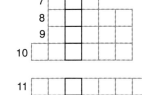
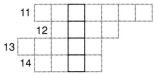
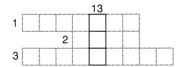

Puzzle B   The words in this puzzle are from Lessons 4–7. Read the sentences below. Then complete the puzzle with the missing words.

1. I was going to have today's special, but I've .... my mind.
2. Look at the .... before you order your meal.
3. I'm going to have shrimp cocktail as an .... .

4. Your father's parents are your .... .
5. A good friend always .... you the truth, even if it hurts.
6. Apple pie is my .... dessert.
7. Your aunt's children are your .... .
8. The main .... of bread are flour, yeast, and water.

9. Although they are divorced, he and his .... are good friends.
10. Your sister's son is your .... .
11. All of your relatives make up your .... .
12. I've known her for a very long time. She is my .... friend.

13. (down) Good friends always ....

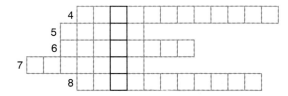
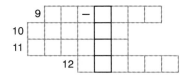

Activity A **1 Pair work** Look at the photos. What job is each person doing?
What would you like and dislike about his or her job? Why?

> I think he/she is . . .   I'd like/I would enjoy doing . . . because . . .
> He/She seems to be . . .   I'd dislike/I wouldn't enjoy doing . . . because . . .

2 Pair work Circle the words below that you don't know and ask
your partner to explain them. Use a dictionary to look up the words that
neither of you knows. Then add the words to the chart.

✔ boss   ✔ pay   health insurance   employee
   retirement plan   freelance position   part-time job   hourly wages
✔ full-time job   employer   raise   temporary position
   supervisor   office worker   manager   overtime pay

People's roles at work	Salary and benefits	Job types
boss	pay	full-time job

1 Listen 🔲 Phil and Christopher are talking to their bosses on the first day of their new jobs. Check (✔) the duties they're told about. Then write the hours they work.

Phil Working hours: . . . . to . . . .

Christopher Working hours: . . . . to . . . .

2 Join a partner Compare your answers. What would *you* enjoy about each job?

3 Listen 🔲 Phil and Christopher are talking about their first day of work. What did they enjoy about their first day? Take notes.

Phil	Christopher
. . . .	. . . .
. . . .	. . . .

4 Join a partner Compare your notes.

Group work Discuss these questions.
- Tell about a job you have had. What did you do? What did you like about the job? What did you dislike?
- What kind of work do you think you'll be doing five years from now?
- What's your ideal job? Give your reasons.
- What's your idea of a terrible job?

In five years I think I'll be working as . . .   My goal is to . . .
I hope to be working as . . .   I'd love/hate to be a . . .

9 An interesting job

1 Read/listen 📼 First read the magazine article and try to guess the missing words. Then listen and check your answers.

walking for a living

a Foley artist at work

A Foley artist earns a living adding sounds like footsteps to movie sound tracks. Footsteps are added in sound studios because when a movie is filmed, the _____ are aimed at the actors' mouths, not their _____ – and because real footsteps just don't sound natural.

A Foley artist watches a _____ in the sound studio and follows the actor's footsteps on a special stage, keeping time with the _____ movements. The Foley artist wears the same kind of shoes that the actor wore and walks on the same surface. For example, if the actor wore boots and _____ on a wood floor, the Foley artist does, too. A skilled Foley artist can match the footsteps exactly to the character the actor is playing and even show _____ like fear or surprise.

Foley artists also add all kinds of sound effects to movies. In a horror film, the sound of _____ breaking is made by snapping celery and dry spaghetti. The sound of burning bodies is created by dripping water onto a hot iron. The sound of horses' hooves used to be made using _____, but modern Foley artists prefer to use a toilet plunger. The sound of _____ is made by scraping an ax across concrete – real ice doesn't sound natural enough.

Jack Foley invented this way of adding _____ _____ to movies in the 1930s. Before that, moviemakers used recordings of sound effects and added them to the movie sound track. Now Foley artists work on almost every movie. The _____ you hear when someone is punched and falls are created by a Foley artist – actors only _____ to hit each other, and their "injuries" are created by makeup artists.

Most Foley artists are very private people. Their work is done in special sound studios, and they don't appear in front of the public or even in front of the _____. And they don't get the appreciation they deserve – if they do the job right, the _____ doesn't even notice.

2 Join a partner Read the article again and answer these questions.

1. What does a Foley artist do?
2. Why are footsteps re-created by Foley artists?
3. What is "artistic" about a Foley artist's footsteps?
4. How is the sound of ice-skating created?
5. How did Foley artists get their name?
6. How much appreciation do Foley artists get? Why?

1 Pair work   The jobs below are related to making movies. Match the jobs to the photos. Can you guess what these people do?

1. cameraperson
2. stuntperson
3. makeup artist
4. animal trainer
5. film editor
6. grip

2 Communication task   Work in groups of three. One of you should look at Task 4 on page C-3, one at Task 11 on page C-7, and one at Task 15 on page C-9. You're going to find out more about some of the jobs above.

Activity C   **Group work**   Discuss these questions.

- Which of the jobs in Activities A and B would you enjoy most? Why?
- Which of the jobs would you enjoy least? Why?
- Would you prefer a nine-to-five job – or a job where the working hours are unpredictable? Give your reasons.
- If you were rich and didn't have to work, would you still want a job? Why or why not?
- Are there any advantages to having a job besides money and benefits? If so, what are they?

10 Useful things

1 Pair work Match the names of these inventions to the pictures.

1. remote control
2. answering machine
3. microwave oven
4. camcorder
5. photocopier
6. mouse
7. clock radio
8. fax machine

2 Pair work Look at these definitions. Which of the useful things on page 22 do you think each one describes? Write the correct number. (There are two extra definitions. Try to guess which items they describe.)

...3... You use it to cook things very quickly.

.... You use it to point at parts of a computer screen.

.... You use it to send a letter or picture to someone very quickly.

.... You use it to clean plates, dishes, glasses, knives, and forks.

.... You use it to take messages when you're away from home.

.... You use it to help you remember vacations and special occasions.

.... You use it to control your TV, VCR, or stereo.

.... You use it to record music or speech and play it back later.

.... You use it to duplicate documents.

.... You use it to wake you up in the morning.

3 Join another pair Discuss these questions.
- Which of the items on page 22 have the greatest influence on your life?
- Which items do you hardly ever use?
- How would your life be different if the items hadn't been invented?

> ... has the greatest influence on my life because ...
> I hardly ever use/I don't own ...
> If ... hadn't been invented, I would have to ...
> If ... hadn't been invented, I wouldn't be able to ...
> Without ..., we'd all have to ...

Activity B **Group work** Choose one of the inventions on page 22. Tell the group how to use it.

> This is how you use the photocopier: First, you put the paper ...

Activity C **Group work** Look at this riddle. What's being described?

I'm found in most people's homes. You can sit on me if you don't have a chair. You can stand on me to reach the ceiling. You can sit under me to get out of the rain. You can even go to sleep on me. What am I?

Think of an object and write a riddle for it. Take turns reading the riddles in your group and guessing the answers to them.

 Before the next lesson, find a small gadget and bring it to class. Keep it in a bag so that the other students can't see it. You will talk about your gadget in Activity C on page 25.

Activity A   **1 Pair work** Look at the pictures in the chart below. What do you think is special about each product?

2 Listen [cassette icon]   You will hear part of a TV show. Complete the chart with the missing information.

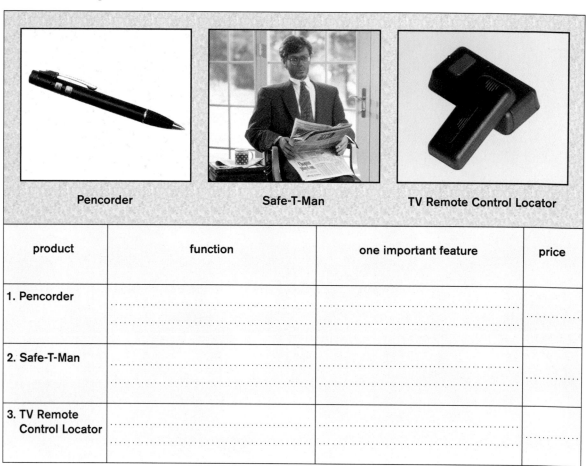

	Pencorder	Safe-T-Man	TV Remote Control Locator

product	function	one important feature	price
1. Pencorder			
2. Safe-T-Man			
3. TV Remote Control Locator			

3 Join a partner Compare your answers. Then discuss these questions.
- Which products sounded very useful to you? not very useful?
- What have you bought in the past few months that you're extremely pleased with? Why?
- What have you bought that you're very disappointed with? Why?

> . . . sounded useful. I'd like to have one of those because . . .
>
> . . . wouldn't be very useful because . . .
>
> I'm very pleased/I'm disappointed with the . . . that I bought because . . .

1 Read/listen 🔲 First read the article about inventors and try to guess the missing words. Then listen and check your answers.

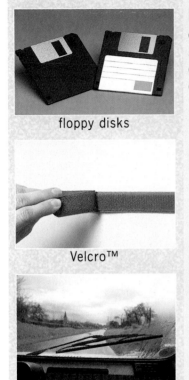

floppy disks

Velcro™

a windshield wiper

YOSHIRO NAKAMATS Dr. Yoshiro Nakamats _____ the first floppy disk in 1950. Nakamats, an _____ at Tokyo University in Japan, holds 2,300 other patents, including one for _____ club designs. IBM, a computer company, bought the sales license for the disks. They _____ Nakamats' design and started selling floppy disks in 1970.

GEORGES DE MESTRAL One day in the 1950s Georges de Mestral was _____ in his native Switzerland, when he noticed some seeds sticking to his jacket. He looked at them under a microscope and saw that the _____ were covered with tiny hooks, which _____ themselves to the fabric of his clothing. This gave him the idea for Velcro™. The first Velcro™ was made by _____ in France and took a long time to make. Today _____ use Velcro™ to prevent objects from _____ around when they are traveling in space.

MARY ANDERSON The windshield wiper was invented in 1903 by Mary Anderson, a woman from Alabama, U.S.A. While Anderson was riding a _____ during a trip to New York City, she noticed that the driver often had to get out to wipe _____ from the windshield. She quickly drew an idea for a windshield wiper in her sketchbook. Later she tried to sell her _____ to a Canadian company, but the company decided that the invention wouldn't be _____. Anderson gave up on trying to sell her _____ and never made any money from it.

Now answer these questions.

Which inventor . . . ?
1. made no money from his/her invention ....
2. invented over 2,000 things ....
3. was inspired on a country walk ....
4. was inspired in the winter ....
5. made an agreement with IBM ....

2 Join a partner Compare your answers. Which invention do you think was the most significant? Why?

> I think that . . . was the most significant because . . .
> . . . is probably a more important invention than . . . because . . .

Group work Keep the gadget you have brought to class in a bag. Each person in the group should describe what's in his or her bag without mentioning the gadget's name. The rest of the group should guess what's being described. Then they should ask why the gadget is useful.

Communication task 🎭 Work in groups of three. One of you should look at Task 5 on page C-4, one at Task 10 on page C-7, and one at Task 16 on page C-10. You're going to talk about some recent inventions.

12 Threats to our environment

Activity A **1 Pair work** Look at these photos. What environmental problem does each picture show? Describe the photos using the words in the box or your own words.

forest
wild animals
tropical
pollution
extinct
endangered species
destruction
wildlife
jungle
smoke

2 Join another pair Compare your answers. Then discuss these questions.
- How do the pictures above make you feel?
- What is the worst environmental problem in your country?
- In your opinion, which of these problems will cause the worst damage to the world? Number the problems from the most serious (1) to the least serious (8).

.... More and more people are living in cities.

.... Rivers and lakes are becoming more polluted.

.... Some plants and animals are becoming extinct.

.... The air in our cities is becoming more polluted.

.... The greenhouse effect is causing the earth's temperature to rise.

.... The population of the world is growing.

.... The fishing industry is depleting our oceans' population of fish.

.... Holes are developing in the ozone layer, the part of the atmosphere that protects the earth from dangerous radiation.

When I look at . . . , I feel . . .
The worst environmental problem in my country is . . .
. . . will cause the most world damage because . . .

1 Read/listen 🔲 First read the article and try to guess the missing words. Then listen and check your answers.

The African Elephant

In 1990, over 100 countries signed an international agreement to make it _____ to buy or sell ivory, which is mainly used for jewelry. Most ivory is made from the tusks of African _____. These tusks are very valuable – one pair is worth more than three times what an African _____ or factory worker earns in a year.

Hunting elephants was so profitable that from 1979 to 1989 the number of elephants in _____ fell from 1.3 million to 600,000. It was feared that by the year 2000 there would be none left. However, since 1990 there has been much less illegal _____, thanks to the international agreement.

But it costs a lot of money to preserve elephants. Game wardens must be hired to _____ them, land must be set aside for them, and when they destroy a farmer's crops, the farmer must be paid compensation.

Zimbabwe and four other African countries say that some of the elephants should be _____ legally. This would help keep the population stable, and selling the ivory would help pay for preserving the elephants. But _____ say that making ivory legal to sell would lead to even more illegal hunting. Others say that it is wrong to kill elephants because they are sensitive animals who feel emotional _____ at the death of other elephants.

What do you think?
- Should the sale of ivory be made legal again?
- Is it right to kill some elephants to save others?
- Should a group of countries be allowed to tell another country what it should do?

Medicinal Plants

When settlers in the United States spread west in the 1800s, they thought nothing of cutting down _____ and killing wildlife to develop their country.

Today, developing countries are cutting down their forests because their people want a better life. But _____ say that this is a disaster. The rain forests are home to half the world's species. Undiscovered rain-forest plants could be used as _____ drugs to treat diseases like AIDS and cancer. Two of today's most powerful anti-cancer medicines come from a single rain-forest _____. Many kinds of plants, which could be the sources of tomorrow's cures, are being destroyed at the rate of 50 to 100 every day.

Developing countries think that it is wrong for people who _____ their own forests long ago to tell them not to develop. They also feel that when a drug company discovers a _____ in their rain forest, the company should share its profits with them.

What do you think?
- Should developing countries have the right to cut down their forests, as the United States did?
- Now that we know the rain forest is an important resource, does the world have the right to tell individual countries what to do with their rain forests?
- Should a drug company share its profits with a developing country when it uses a rain-forest plant as a medicine – even if the country did nothing to research, develop, and market the drug?

Now look at the "What do you think?" box after each reading and answer the questions.

2 Group work Compare your answers. Do you have the same opinions?

> I agree/I don't agree with you because . . .   You have a point, but . . .
> I understand your point, but . . .

Activity A

1 Work alone How green are you? Take the quiz and find out. Give each item a number from 1 to 5.

1 = always   2 = often   3 = sometimes   4 = hardly ever   5 = never

How GREEN are you?

Do you . . . ?

1. avoid throwing things away if they can be reused, repaired, or recycled	
2. use recycled paper	
3. make sure the paper, glass, and cans you throw away will be recycled	
4. avoid products from nonrenewable sources (e.g., wood from tropical rain forests)	
5. avoid buying overpackaged products	
6. use a bike or walk when traveling short distances	
7. use public transportation when traveling long distances	
8. avoid or turn down the air-conditioning in the summer	
9. make sure the heat isn't turned up too high in the winter	
10. use low-energy light bulbs	
11. turn off the lights when you leave a room	
12. avoid using more water than you need	

2 Join a partner Compare your answers to the quiz. Do you and your partner do the same things? Who is more "green"?

3 Join another pair Discuss these questions.
- What do you think is the most important thing to do listed in the quiz?
- What do you think is the least important thing?
- Is recycling popular in your country? Why or why not?
- What recycling programs are available at your school? in your city or town?

The most/least important thing to do in the quiz is . . .
Recycling is/isn't popular in my country because . . .

Activity B   **1 Listen** 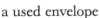 Five people are talking about recycling these items. Listen and write down the item each person is talking about. Then write one way the item can be recycled.

a used envelope   old reports   an empty container   a chipped cup   used aluminum foil

Item	One way to recycle
1. *old reports*	*use them for note paper*
2.	
3.	
4.	
5.	

2 Join a partner   Compare your answers. Then discuss these questions.
- Which of the ideas in the recording seemed the best to you? the worst?
- Can you think of any other ideas for recycling things or avoiding waste?

3 Group work   Look at the photos and discuss these questions.
- What is happening in each photo?
- What benefits to the environment do you see in each photo?

Activity C   **Communication task**  Work with a partner. One of you should look at Task 8 on page C-6, and the other at Task 17 on page C-10. You're going to talk about environmental problems and solutions.

Activity A **1 Pair work** Look at these pictures of vacations. Which vacation looks the most enjoyable? Which looks like the least fun?

2 Listen 📼 Four people are describing their vacations. Write the number of the description on the correct picture.

3 Listen again 📼 Who is describing his or her vacation? Look at the chart and check (✔) the correct column.

Who . . . ?	Wanda	Robert	Marni	Tom
didn't miss his/her family				
didn't enjoy doing the chores				
expected to be bored – but wasn't				
went to the zoo				
got wet and scared				
missed his/her friends				
picked fruit				
enjoyed watching the stars				
studied				
thinks the country is too quiet				
walked 200 miles in a week				
went jogging or swimming every day				
went to the opera				
wishes he/she had planned ahead better				

4 Join a partner Discuss these questions.
- Now that you know more about what the people did on their vacations, have you changed your answers to Activity A1? Why or why not?
- What's the nicest vacation you have taken? Tell your partner about it.

> *(Wanda's) vacation sounded really enjoyable/awful because . . .*
> *The nicest vacation I've ever taken was when I . . .*

Activity B **Group work** Look at the photos and discuss these questions.
- What are the people doing? Where do you think they are?
- Imagine that you could take one of these vacations. Which one would you choose? Why?
- If your dream vacation isn't shown here, describe it to the group.

Activity C **Communication task** Divide into an even number of pairs. Half the pairs should look at Task 6 on page C-4, and the other half at Task 9 on page C-6. You're going to look at some vacation snapshots.

Activity A

1 Pair work Look at the chart below and discuss these questions.

- In which country do people travel the most by car? bus? train? air? In which country do people travel the least by these forms of transportation?
- What do you think are the reasons for the differences?
- Do you take any of the forms of transportation below? Which ones? Where do you take them?

KILOMETERS TRAVELED PER PERSON PER YEAR

	by car	by bus	by train	by air
Brazil	3,600	NA*	110	185
France	10,400	780	1,131	919
Japan	4,400	900	1,923	746
South Korea	20,311	560	698	428
UK	10,100	740	583	1,845
USA	16,400	150	80	2,775

*NA = not available

1.6 kilometers = 1 mile

> People in . . . travel the most/least by . . .
> Trains are popular in Japan because . . .
> When I go to work, I usually . . .

2 Join another pair Tell the group how you get to class. Who has the most difficult trip? the easiest? Who takes more than one form of transportation?

3 Group work Imagine you're the people in these photos. How would you feel in each situation? What would you do? What do you think is going to happen next?

Activity B   **Group work**   Discuss these questions.
- What kinds of cars are the most popular in your country?
- Do you think a car says something about its driver? What kind of person typically owns each of these cars?

a family sedan

a minivan

a sports car

a classic car

a limousine

a jeep

- Do you know what these types of cars look like? Describe each one.

| a station wagon | a pickup truck | a convertible | a hatchback |

- Imagine that you could have any car you want. What would it be?
- Have you ever taken driving lessons? a driving test? Describe the experience.

> If I could have any car, I would get a . . . because . . .
> I think a rich/adventurous/married person would probably own a . . .
> When I took my first driving lesson, I was scared/nervous/excited . . .

Before the next lesson, bring one of these items to class.
- some photographs or postcards of a vacation or a weekend trip
- an unusual souvenir you brought back from a trip
- a gift someone brought back for you from a vacation

You will talk about the item in Activity D on page 36.

16 What's it like there?

1 Pair work Look at these photos. Describe each scene using the words in the box or your own words. Which country or countries do you think they show?

skyscrapers
coast
mountains
desert
cliffs
beach
sailboats
rocks
surf
sand

2 Join another pair Compare your ideas. Then discuss these questions.
- Which of the pictures above looks the most interesting to you? Why?
- Have you ever visited another country? What did you like about it? What did you dislike?
- If you could visit another country, where would you go? Why?

The second picture looks the most interesting because . . .
I went to . . . three years ago. I loved the beaches, but I didn't like . . .
If I could visit another country, I'd go to . . . because . . .
I'd love to visit . . .

1 Listen 📼 Jackie, Nick, and Kate are talking about countries they have visited. First read the questions below. Then listen and write the answers. Guess which country each person is talking about.

1 Jackie

1. What was the weather like? ....

2. What did she like the most about her trip? ....

3. What was her favorite place? Why? ....

4. What country do you think Jackie is talking about? ....

2 Nick

1. What did Nick do during the first part of his trip? ....

2. What did he like the most about his trip? ....

3. Why would he go back? ....

4. What country do you think Nick is talking about? ....

3 Kate

1. What was the weather like? ....

2. What did Kate like the most about her trip? ....

3. What did she buy in Taxco? ....

4. What country do you think Kate is talking about? ....

2 Group work Discuss these questions.
- What are the most popular tourist attractions in your country?
- What cities or regions in your country do most tourists visit? Would you tell a foreign friend to go there on vacation? Why or why not?
- Besides sight-seeing, what can a tourist do to get a really authentic experience of your country?

1 Read/listen 📼 First read the advertisement and try to guess the missing words. Then listen and check your answers.

This is what New Zealand looks like to the experienced traveler.

A _____ traveler who tries to describe New Zealand is apt to paint an extraordinary _____. He'll begin by telling you it has the unspoiled _____ of Alaska, beaches that rival Hawaii, breathtakingly _____ fjords like Norway, and majestic Alps like Switzerland. Then, to confuse things a little more, he'll tell you New Zealand's cities and _____ will make you think of England, New Zealand's lush green _____ will remind you of Ireland, and her towering Mt. Egmont will bring to mind Japan's Mt. Fuji. To top it off, he'll say New Zealand has the _____ people, fairest climate, and _____ air on all the green earth. And on all counts, he'll be right. For the full story about New Zealand's diversity, _____ in this coupon.

Please send me more details.

Name_____

Address_____

New Zealand Tourist Office,
New Zealand House,
Haymarket,
London SW1Y 4TQ

New Zealand
One-Stop World Tour

2 Pair work Discuss these questions.
- How many different places are mentioned in the advertisement? What are the places mentioned famous for?
- Do you think this advertisement encourages people to visit New Zealand? Why or why not?
- How is New Zealand similar to your country? How is it different?

3 Pair work Think of three countries that were not in the advertisement. Write two or three things you associate with each country.

Country	Things associated with the country

Group work Show the vacation photographs, postcards, souvenir, or gift that you brought to class today. Tell the group the story behind your item(s).

Communication task 😀😀 Work in groups of four. Two of you should look at Task 7 on page C-5, and the other two at Task 18 on page C-11. You're going to learn about about some English-speaking countries.

Review puzzles

Puzzle A The words in this puzzle are from Lessons 8–13. Read the sentences below. Then complete the puzzle with the missing words.

1. A Foley artist adds sound .... to movies.
2. He doesn't have a job; he's .... .
3. Yoshiro Nakamats is an .... .
4. Another word for boss is .... .
5. It's not a permanent job. It's only .... .
6. If you work for someone else, you are an .... .
7. Smoke from factories is an example of air .... .
8. A .... control operates a TV.
9. Bottles and cans can be .... .
10. Every day more and more plants and animals are becoming .... .
11. At a job interview, you can ask about the salary and .... insurance.

12. (down) We must all do what we can to protect the .... .

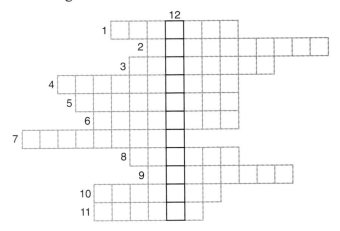

Puzzle B The words in this puzzle are from Lessons 14–16. Read the sentences below. Then complete the puzzle with the missing words.

1. Where did you go on .... last summer?
2. Buses and trains are forms of public .... .
3. A typical family car is a .... .
4. A millionaire probably rides in a .... .
5. A world .... has visited many different countries.
6. When I visit a new place, I go .... . I visit all of the famous museums and monuments.
7. When you are visiting another country, you are a .... .
8. I love to go to the .... and swim in the ocean.
9. I bought a model of the Statue of Liberty as a .... of New York.
10. A .... is a very tall building.
11. When people go on vacation, they often mail .... to their family and friends.
12. I don't like cities. I prefer the .... .
13. We're taking a .... to Australia next month.
14. A .... is a hot, dry place with few plants and animals.
15. I hate having to help out around the house and do .... .
16. What are the main tourist .... of the city?

17. (down) VCR stands for video ....

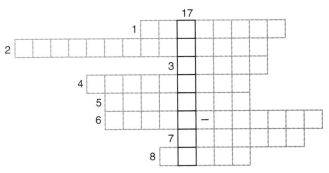

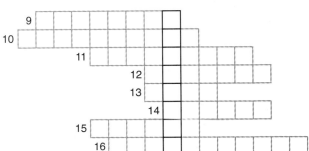

Activity A **1 Pair work** What are the leisure activities shown in these pictures? Which of them do you enjoy doing and why?

2 Listen Four people are talking about their favorite leisure activities. As you listen, complete the first column of the chart with the activities pictured above.

	Favorite hobbies or interests?	What do you enjoy most about each activity?	How long do you spend on each activity?
Wanda	1.		
	2.		
Robert	1.		
	2.		
Christopher	1.		
	2.		
Sheila	1.		
	2.		

3 Listen again What do these people enjoy most about their activities, and how much time do they spend on them? Complete the second and third columns of the chart above.

1 Pair work Look at the photos and discuss these questions.
● What are the people doing?
● Would you like to be doing the same thing? Why or why not?

2 Work alone Decide which of your interests gives you the most enjoyment. Write down some of the reasons why you enjoy it so much.

3 Join a partner Ask your partner these questions.
● If you only had time for one of your hobbies or interests, what would it be?
● Why do you enjoy it so much?
● Would you like to spend more time on it? Why?

I really enjoy . . . because . . .
I wish I had more time to spend on . . . because . . .

Communication task Work with a partner. One of you should look at Task 19 on page C-12, and the other at Task 29 on page C-17. You're going to talk about hobbies.

Activity A   **1 Pair work**   If a lifetime could be compressed into a week, this is how much time a person would spend doing these things.

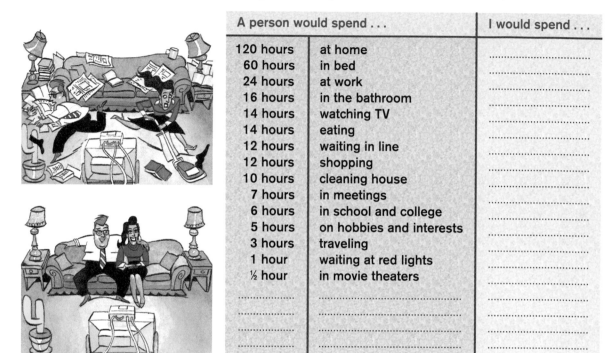

A person would spend . . .		I would spend . . .
120 hours	at home	....
60 hours	in bed	....
24 hours	at work	....
16 hours	in the bathroom	....
14 hours	watching TV	....
14 hours	eating	....
12 hours	waiting in line	....
12 hours	shopping	....
10 hours	cleaning house	....
7 hours	in meetings	....
6 hours	in school and college	....
5 hours	on hobbies and interests	....
3 hours	traveling	....
1 hour	waiting at red lights	....
½ hour	in movie theaters	....
....	....	....
....	....	....
....	....	....

Discuss which statistics are most surprising – or unbelievable.

> I can't believe that people spend 12 hours a week shopping.
> It's hard to believe that . . .
> It's surprising/It doesn't surprise me that . . .
> Do you think that people really spend . . . ?

2 Work alone   Look at the chart again. What important activities are missing? Add them to the list.

3 Pair work   In a typical week, how many hours do you spend doing each activity? Fill in the column on the right and compare your answers with your partner.

> Studying isn't in the chart – I spend two hours studying every day.
> You spend more time eating than I do.
> I think I spend more time watching TV than the average person.

1 Pair work Complete this chart with your partner.
- Add three more of your own leisure activities at the end of the list.
- Approximately how many times have you and your partner done each activity in the past month?
- If you had more leisure time, how would you spend it?

How many times do you...?

	You	Your partner		You	Your partner
watch a sports game	....	....	go to a café or bar	....	....
play a sport	....	....	read a book	....	....
play cards	....	....	read a magazine	....	....
play a computer game	....	....	listen to music	....	....
watch a video	....	....	go shopping	....	....
watch television	....	....	eat out	....	....
go to the movies	....	....	prepare a meal	....	....
go for a walk	....	....	....	....	....
visit a museum	....	....	....	....	....
go dancing	....	....	....	....	....

> I've watched a sports game three times this month.
> I've played basketball twice in the past month.
> If I had more time, I would . . .

2 Join another pair Compare your leisure activities with theirs. In what ways are you the same? different?

> . . . eats out more often than I do.
> . . . likes reading books more than I do, but I read more magazines than he/she does.
> . . . visits museums more often than any of us, and he/she says that he/she never watches TV!

19 Playing and watching sports

Activity A

1 Pair work Look at these photos. Describe each picture using the words in the box or your own words. What is happening? What's going to happen next?

energetic
exciting
dangerous
surfer
go surfing
runner
run a race
volleyball player
play volleyball
competition
win
lose
score

2 Join another pair Compare your ideas. Then discuss these questions.
- Why do you think each of these sports is popular?
- Which sport do you think is the most exciting? Why?
- What are the dangers of each sport?
- Have you participated in any of these sports? Would you like to? Why or why not?
- Do you like to play sports? Why or why not?

> I've played/gone/run . . .
> I'd like to/I don't think I'd like to . . .
> I love playing/I don't like playing . . .
> I love to play/I don't like to play . . .

1 Listen 🔲 Six people are talking about what they do to stay in shape. The speakers mention several advantages of each healthy practice. Write just one advantage.

	Advantages
1. Lori does yoga.	*calming*
2. Terry goes swimming.	
3. Robert runs.	
4. Trevor walks everywhere.	
5. Christopher plays basketball.	
6. Bill follows a vegetarian diet.	

2 Join a partner Compare your answers. Then discuss these questions.
- Of the six people on the recording, whose ideas do you agree with most? least? Why?
- What do *you* do to keep healthy and stay in shape?

1 Pair work Look at the sports listed below. Which of these sports follow the word *play*? the word *go*? the word *do*? Write *play, go,* or *do* next to each sport.

Sports Quiz

	Participate in	Watch		Participate in	Watch		Participate in	Watch		Participate in	Watch
do aerobics			.... football			.... judo			.... surfing		
.... badminton			.... golf			.... karate			.... swimming		
.... baseball			.... gymnastics			.... rock climbing			.... tennis		
.... basketball			.... hockey			.... roller-skating			.... volleyball		
.... bowling			.... horseback riding			.... sailing			.... walking		
.... cycling			.... ice-skating			.... skiing			.... weight lifting		
.... fishing			.... jogging			.... soccer			.... windsurfing		

Total

2 Work alone Are you a "sports nut"? Take the quiz and find out. Follow these instructions.

1. How many times a year do you participate in each sport? Write the number in the *Participate in* column of the quiz.
2. How many times a year do you watch other people participate in each sport? Write the number in the *Watch* column of the quiz.

3 Join a partner Turn to Task 34 on page C-20 to find out your score. Then discuss these questions.
- Was the quiz right about you? How much of a "sports nut" do *you* think you are?
- Which of your favorite sports are missing from the list?

20 How about a game?

1 Pair work Look at the picture. Then discuss the questions below.

- Which of these games do you recognize?
- Which do you know how to play?
- Which game do you enjoy playing most? Why?

2 Pair work Look at this list and add the names of your own favorite games.

Board games	chess shogi checkers Monopoly Scrabble
Card games	bridge poker rummy solitaire hanafuda
Tile games	dominoes mah-jongg
Word games	crossword puzzles word-search puzzles hangman
Party games	charades musical chairs
Computer games	Tetris Doom

Ask your partner these questions.
- Which of the games in the list above are familiar to you?
- Which do you like to play?
- Which games don't you play anymore? Why did you give them up?

> I know how to play . . .
> I don't know much about . . .
> I like to play . . .
> I don't play . . . anymore because . . .

1 Group work Read these descriptions of some popular word games. Then choose one game to play in your group.

"I went on a trip . . ."

Each player has to remember the list of things started by the previous player and add one more item to the list. For example:

A: I went on a trip and took *an umbrella*.

B: I went on a trip and took *an umbrella* and *a guidebook*.

C: I went on a trip and took *an umbrella*, *a guidebook*, and *my sister*.

The first player to make a mistake has to start a new list.

Endings and beginnings

One player says a word. The next player has to say a word beginning with the letter that ended the previous word. For example:

A: apple

B: elephant

C: tomato

D: only

If the next player can't think of a word or gets the letter wrong, he or she is out of the game. The winner is the last one to give a correct word.

"I love my love with an A . . ."

The first player begins like this: I love my love with an *A* because he/she is *adorable*.

The second player continues: I love my love with a *B* because he/she is *adorable* and *brave*.

The third continues: I love my love with a *C* because he/she is *adorable* and *brave* and *clever*.

This goes on through the alphabet until someone can't remember or can't think of a word. Then the game starts again from the letter where it went wrong, *not* from the letter *A*.

"Who am I?"

One person leaves the room. The others in the group think of a famous person, real or fictional, living or dead. The person who left the room returns and asks, "Who am I?" Each person in the group has to answer the question with a clue. For example:

A: Who am I?

B: You're a movie star.

A: Who am I?

C: You're very good-looking.

A: Who am I?

D: You have blond hair.

When each person in the group has been asked, the guesser has three chances to guess the famous person. If he or she is wrong, the others reveal the answer. Then another person leaves the room and the game begins again.

Word associations

One player says a word. Then, without hesitating, the next player has to say another word that the first word brings to mind. If someone hesitates (or says a word that is *not* associated in any way), he or she drops out. The game continues until just one player is left. For example:

A: vacation

B: photograph

C: camera

D: movie

E: star

F: sun

2 Group work Choose a second game to play. Then compare your experiences with the rest of the class. Which games did you like best? least? Why?

Communication task Work in groups of three. One of you should look at Task 24 on page C-15, one at Task 28 on page C-16, and one at Task 33 on page C-19. Each of you is going to imagine that you're a famous person.

21 In the news

Activity A **1 Pair work**   Look at these news photos. What is happening? Describe each photo using the words in the box or your own words.

burn
emotional
firefighter
whale
happy
ocean
helicopter
rescue
flames
reunion

2 Join another pair   Compare your ideas. What do you think each news story is about? What happened before and after each photo was taken?

It looks as if . . .
This is what happened: . . .
Just before this picture was taken, . . .
The next thing that happened was . . .

Activity B

1 Listen 🔲 You will hear part of a news broadcast. Match the news stories to the pictures in Activity A1. Number the pictures from 1 to 4.

2 Listen again 🔲 Complete the summaries of the news stories.

1. Strong .... drove forest fire .... towards the city of Bellevue. Hundreds of .... had to leave their homes. The fire is now under ....

2. Mary Avona was .... from a boat by helicopter and taken to the .... She had an .... to remove her appendix. Doctors say the operation was a ....

3. A whale was unable to return to the .... Over the weekend, sight-seers .... the whale. Divers were able to calm the whale down and .... it to the open ocean.

4. Stacy Baxter met her .... sister, Alicia Carson, for the first time. They were .... at birth and .... by different families.

3 Group work Compare your summaries. Which story had the happiest ending?

Activity C

1 Pair work Think of three countries that have been in the news recently. What events have put them in the news?

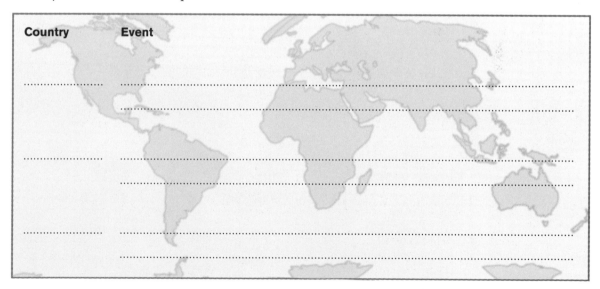

Country	Event
....	....
....	....
....	....
....	....

2 Join another pair Compare your ideas. Did you think of the same places and events – or different ones?

 Before the next lesson, find one or two amusing or interesting short news articles from a newspaper or magazine – preferably an English-language one. You will talk about the articles in Activity D on page 50.

22 Keep up to date!

1 Work alone Complete the questionnaire.

THE NEWS & CURRENT EVENTS

1. How do you learn about the news? Write O (*Often*), S (*Sometimes*), or N (*Never*).
   .... radio   .... weekly newsmagazine
   .... TV   .... other (please specify)
   .... daily newspaper

2. When you read a newspaper, which sections do you read? Which do you usually ignore? Write R (*Read*) or I (*Ignore*).
   .... world news   .... weather
   .... national news (about your country)   .... arts
   .... local news (about your city/town)   .... comics
   .... business news   .... other (please specify)
   .... sports

3. What recent news story has upset you most?
   ....

4. What recent news story or event amused or pleased you most?
   ....

5. Do you think it's important to keep up to date about the news? Why?
   ....

6. Name one controversial news issue that interests you.
   ....

2 Group work Compare your answers. What do you have in common with your group? How are you different?

> I usually read/watch/listen to . . .
> One of the worst things that has happened recently is . . .
> I was very upset by . . .
> One of the funniest/nicest things that has happened recently is . . .
> I really enjoyed the story about . . .
> I'm very interested in . . .
> I have strong feelings about . . .

---

① *WALKMAN REVENGE*

A _____ commuter in England was so angry at the _____ coming from a young man's Walkman that he took a pair of scissors from his _____ and cut through the headphone wire. His fellow _____ applauded.

---

② **TIME IS MONEY**

A woman in Chicago was very _____ when her ex-husband remarried. While he and his new wife were on their _____, she broke into his apartment and _____ the "speaking clock" in London for the time. She left the phone off the hook and went home. The phone was off the hook until the _____ got back from vacation two weeks later. The phone _____ came to over $8,000.

---

③ **VIRTUAL BABY**

For people who like _____ but don't have the time for a family, Quality Video of Minneapolis, Minnesota, U.S.A., has _____ "Video Baby." This 30-minute tape shows two babies doing what babies do, like crawl around the house, _____ with a rattle, take a bubble bath, and turn _____ into a complete mess. There's no narrator, so once the _____ is in the VCR, there's nothing to come between the viewer and the baby but the _____ button.

Of course, some things are left out, like babies _____ and spitting up, not to mention the _____ of a full diaper. As the package says, "Enjoy bath time without being _____, mealtime without wearing the food." Sound good? Imagine the possibilities for "Video Teenager."

---

④ **Free Trip to the U.S.**

Two Irish boys went to New York last week after their mothers told them not to play far from home because _____ was almost ready. They traveled without _____ from Dublin to London – and then on to New York's Kennedy Airport.

Noel Murray, aged 13, and Keith Byrne, 10, were picked up by the _____ outside Kennedy Airport because they looked "tired and _____."

The youths were flown _____ to their parents yesterday. Keith's mother, Teresa, said to reporters: "I told him not to go far."

"We didn't really _____ what we wanted to do when we got there," Keith said last night. "We got off the _____ with the other people, but we didn't see much of New York."

The trip is the boys' second _____ to see the world this month. Two weeks ago they were caught on board a _____ to England and sent home to their parents.

---

2 Join a partner Discuss these questions.
- Which story is the most interesting? Why?
- Which is the most upsetting? Why?
- Which is the most amusing? Why?

3 Pair work Write a one-sentence summary of each story. Begin like this: "This story is about . . ."

4 Join another pair Compare your answers to the questions. Then compare your summaries.

Activity C   **Pair work**   Discuss these questions.
- Do you believe everything you hear on the news or read in the newspapers? Why or why not?
- If you hear an eyewitness being interviewed about an event, do you usually believe him or her? Why or why not?

Activity D   **Group work**   Tell your group about the news articles you brought to class today. Tell the stories in your own words.

Activity E   **Communication task**   👀   Study the photo below for ten seconds only. Then look at Task 25 on page C-15. You're going to answer questions about the picture.

Review puzzles

Puzzle A The words in this puzzle are from Lessons 17–20. Read the sentences below. Then complete the puzzle with the missing words.

1. The final .... of the soccer game was 3 to 1.
2. Sheila's .... is making jewelry.
3. Baseball is the most .... sport in the United States.
4. No one likes to .... a game.
5. The activities that you do in your free time are .... activities.
6. Hang gliding and rock .... are dangerous sports.
7. Soccer isn't usually played indoors. It's played .... .
8. .... is a card game you can play on your own.
9. She's a .... . She doesn't eat meat.
10. .... is a calming and relaxing leisure activity.

11. (down) Some people spend their leisure time .... things like stamps.

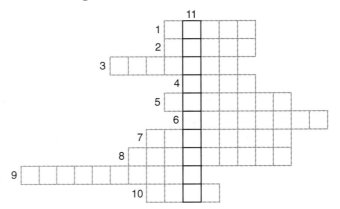

Puzzle B The words in this puzzle are from Lessons 21–22. Read the sentences below. Then complete the puzzle with the missing words.

1. News about your city is .... news.
2. News from abroad is .... news.
3. News about your country is .... news.
4. Read the .... section of the newspaper to find out tomorrow's temperature.
5. The result of the basketball game is in the .... section of the newspaper.
6. The .... always make me laugh.
7. There are many ways to learn about the news. You can listen to the radio, read the newspaper, or watch .... .
8. The forest fire .... came close to the city.
9. Every evening the news .... tells you about important events of the day.
10. A woman was .... from a sailboat by helicopter.
11. Did you hear about the .... who were reunited after 45 years?
12. Yesterday a team of divers guided a .... out of the bay and into the ocean.
13. There's an interesting .... about Japanese artists in the paper today.

14. (down) The death penalty is a very .... issue.

Activity A

1 Pair work These photos show city life. Describe each scene using the words in the box or your own words.

commuters
recreation
mass transit
subway
fun
nightlife
park
unpleasant
exercise
relaxation

2 Listen 🔲 Kevin lives in the country. Jeffrey lives in the city. They both talk about the advantages of where they live. Take notes on what Kevin and Jeffrey say.

Advantages of city life	Advantages of country life
interesting, good jobs	*quieter*

3 Join a partner Compare your notes. Then discuss these questions.
- What are some more advantages of living in the city? in the country?
- Where would *you* prefer to live? Why?
- Think about the city or town where you live. What do you like most about it?
- What don't you like about it?
- What are two words you would use to describe it?

1 Pair work Look at the chart. Then answer the questions below.

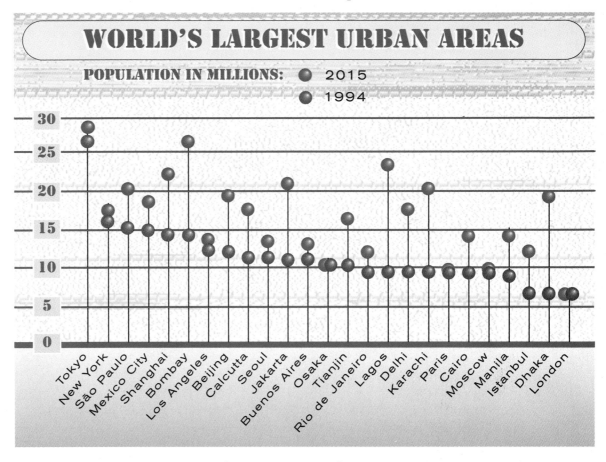

1. Which city will grow the most from 1994 to 2015?
2. Which cities will stay the same size?
3. How many cities had over 10 million inhabitants in 1994?
4. According to the chart, which regions of the world have the fastest growing cities?
5. Does any of the information in the chart surprise you? Why or why not?

2 Group work Discuss these questions with your partners.
- What's the largest city you have ever been to? What was it like there?
- What's your favorite city to visit? Why?
- If you could choose a city to live in, which would it be? Why?

The largest city I've been to is . . .
I love visiting . . . because . . .
I really like to visit . . .
I'd love to live in . . .

Activity C **Communication task** Work with a partner. One of you should look at Task 23 on page C-14, and the other at Task 31 on page C-18. You're going to look at some information about different cities around the world.

24 Safety and crime

1 Work alone Fill out this questionnaire about things you do to avoid crime. Which of these things do you do? Which of these things do you avoid doing? Check (✔) the things you do.

Do you . . . ?	Do you avoid . . . ?
☐ carry a flashlight or a personal alarm	☐ wearing jewelry on the street
☐ keep car doors locked at traffic lights	☐ making eye contact with strangers
☐ carry only a small amount of cash	☐ taking public transportation late at night
☐ carry only one credit card	☐ talking to strangers
☐ walk only on well-lit streets	☐ going out alone at night

2 Join a partner Compare your answers. Do you do the same things to avoid crime? How are you different?

> We both avoid making eye contact with strangers.
> Neither of us carries a flashlight.
> I avoid wearing jewelry on the street, but you don't.

Activity B

1 Listen 🔲 Three people are talking about crime and safety where they live. Who is talking? Look at the chart and check (✔) the correct column.

Who . . . ?	Larry	Anne	Paul
stands near other people while waiting for the subway			
has locks on the windows of his/her apartment			
avoids making eye contact with people on the street			
has his/her apartment keys ready			
doesn't walk alone late at night			
doesn't let strangers into his/her apartment building			
rides in the subway car with the conductor late at night			
always looks like he/she knows where he/she's going			
tells his/her roommate where he/she's going			

2 Join a partner Compare your answers. Do you do any of the things that the people mentioned? Which ones?

3 Group work Discuss these questions.
- Do you worry about crime and safety where you live? when you travel to another city or country?
- What things do you do to stay safe?

> I worry/I don't worry about crime because . . .
> My city is/isn't dangerous . . .
>
> To stay safe, I always/never . . .
> This is what I do to stay safe: . . .

Activity C **1 Pair work** Look at the chart. Then discuss the questions below.

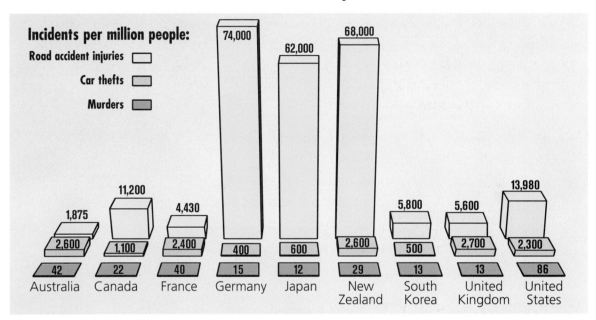

- Which country is the most dangerous?
- Which is the safest?
- How safe is your country? If it's not in the chart, how do you think it compares to the countries listed in the chart?

2 Group work Read these descriptions. Which do you think really are crimes? Number the list from 1 (the most serious) to 8 (the least serious).

.... A couple stole food because they were hungry and had no money.

.... A group of young men started fighting with each other. No one else was involved.

.... A person rode the subway without paying.

.... Some teenagers painted graffiti on the wall of a building.

.... A person threw away an empty coffee cup on the sidewalk.

.... An office worker took home pens and stationery for personal use.

.... A politician was paid a lot of money by a businessman.

.... A gang member was shot by a member of his own gang.

25 Yes, but is it art?

Activity A   **1 Pair work**   Look at these works of art and find out your partner's reactions to each one. Use the words in the box or your own words to talk about each picture.

painting/sculpture
abstract/figurative
realistic/nonrealistic/surrealistic
bright colors/dark colors
portrait/still life/landscape

2 Join another pair   Compare your reactions. Then discuss these questions.

- Which work of art above do you like best? least? Why?
- What kind of art do you like? Do you prefer painting or sculpture? abstract art or realistic art? modern art or traditional art?
- Do you have a favorite artist? Who is it? Why do you like his or her art?

I like . . . the best/the least because . . .   I like . . . art because . . .
I like how the artist shows . . .   I prefer . . . to . . . because . . .

3 Class activity Discuss these questions.

- The works of the artists below appear on page 56. Do you recognize any of these names? If so, tell the class what you know about the artist.
- Can you match these artists to their art? (The answers are on page C-20.)

Xu Beihong (1895–1953)
known for traditional paintings of horses

Piet Mondrian (1872–1944)
known for abstract paintings that use horizontal and vertical blocks of bright colors

Fernando Botero (1932–   )
known for figurative paintings and sculptures of heavy, muscular people

Georgia O'Keeffe (1887–1986)
known for realistic still lifes of flowers

Frida Kahlo (1910–1954)
known for surrealistic self-portraits

Nicolas Poussin (1593–1665)
known for realistic landscapes

Activity B **Group work** Discuss these questions.

- In your opinion, when can these be considered "works of art"? Which could never be "works of art"?

    a building   a piece of pottery   clothing

- Would you ever consider *these* to be works of art? When?

    a novel   a movie   a meal

- Would you ever consider these people to be great artists? In what circumstances?

    an actor   a comedian   a singer

> . . . is a work of art when . . .
> . . . could never be a work of art because . . .
> An actor is a great artist if . . .

Activity C **Communication task** Work in pairs. Both of you should look at Task 27 on page C-16. You're going to talk about paintings.

Activity A
1 Pair work Which photos show things you enjoy? Which photos show things you don't enjoy? Put the photos in order of preference. Then explain your reasons.

2 Pair work Work with a partner you haven't worked with recently. Use this questionnaire to find out about his or her interests. Before you begin, discuss any words that you don't know with your partner.

Questionnaire

1. **Do you ever go to these events? How often?**

   the opera ....   a ballet ....   a rock concert ....

   the symphony ....   a movie ....   a play ....

2. **What kinds of music do you enjoy listening to?** ....

3. **What kinds of books do you like to read?** ....

4. **If you could only have one form of entertainment, what would it be? Why?** ....
   ....

3 Class activity Report your findings to the class. Tell the class one thing that you have in common with your partner and one way that you're different.

> *. . . goes to . . . once a week/once a month/all the time.*
> *He/She never/hardly ever goes to . . .*
> *We both enjoy/We don't enjoy . . .*

Activity B   **1 Pair work**   Look at the words below. Which would you use to describe an event you liked? Which would you use to describe an event you didn't like? Put the words in the correct column.

✔terrible   awful   horrible   exciting   hilarious   thrilling
brilliant   disappointing   funny   violent   offensive   clever

Positive words		Negative words	
....	....	...*terrible*............	....
....	....	....	....
....	....	....	....

Add two words to each column in the chart.

2 Read/listen   First read the movie review and try to guess the missing words. Then listen and check your answers.

MEET THE APPLEGATES

The Applegates are a clean-living model American _____ . Father Dick is a security man at a power plant. Mother Jane is a housewife. _____ Sally and Johnny are great kids. But what no one knows is that the Applegates are really _____ ! They come from the Amazon rain _____ and have disguised themselves as humans so that they can start a campaign to stop people from _____ their home.

While they're _____ their campaign, the Applegates try to make friends and act like a normal family (which isn't easy since they only eat _____ and liquid sugar!). But they soon have _____ . Jane starts charging too much on her new _____ cards, and Johnny becomes friends with a _____ crowd of heavy-metal fans. Sally gets pregnant, and Dick falls in love with another woman. But thankfully Aunt Bea Applegate arrives to _____ the day!

Packed with _____ special effects, witty observations, and plenty of _____ , *Meet the Applegates* is a _____ film with an environmental theme.

3 Join a partner   Tell your partner two reasons why you would want to see this film and two reasons why you wouldn't.

4 Group work   Discuss these questions.
- Who are your two favorite female and two favorite male movie stars? Why do you like them? What are their best movies?
- Think of some movies that you have seen recently. Which movie do you recommend? Tell your group the story without giving away the ending. Use some of the words in Activity B1 in your description.
- Who's your favorite movie director? What are his or her best films?

> You really ought to see . . . because . . .   I really liked . . .
> The movie is about a man/woman who . . .   It's a story about . . .

1 Listen 🔳 You will hear a tune recorded in five different musical styles. As you listen, give each example a score from 1 to 5.

> 1 = This is great! I love this kind of music.
> 2 = This is good music.
> 3 = This music is OK, but it's not my favorite.
> 4 = I don't like this kind of music very much.
> 5 = I hate this kind of music.

1. ....   2. ....   3. ....   4. ....   5. ....

2 Listen again 🔳 Match each piece of music to these descriptions.

country and western ....   jazz ....   classical ....

easy listening ....   heavy metal ....

3 Join a partner Discuss these questions.
- Compare your musical tastes with your partner's. What kinds of music do you enjoy that you did not hear in the recording? Can you add three more kinds of music to the list above?
- What are the names of these instruments?

4 Join another pair Compare your answers. Then discuss these questions.
- What's your favorite kind of music? Why do you like it?
- Who are your two favorite composers?
- What's your favorite band or group?
- Who's your favorite male singer? female singer?
- What's your favorite song? Why do you like it?
- What instruments do you know how to play? What instruments would you like to be able to play?

> I love ... because ...
> I like to listen to ... because ...
> I really love that song because ...
> I don't know why people like ...
> I'd like to learn how to play ...

Review puzzles

Puzzle A The words in this puzzle are from Lessons 23–24. Read the sentences below. Then complete the puzzle with the missing words.

1. If the .... lights are red, drivers have to stop.
2. To be safe, put .... on the windows of your apartment.
3. Usually, there are more .... than houses in a city.
4. How much does it cost to .... on a bus in your city?

5. The fastest way to travel around a big city is by .... .
6. If you are walking alone late at night, don't carry a lot of .... .
7. .... are people who travel to work by bus or train.
8. Some cities have exciting .... . There are a lot of restaurants, dance clubs, and jazz clubs.
9. Not all cities are .... places. Some cities are very safe.
10. I never talk to .... on the subway late at night.
11. To be safe, don't walk .... late at night.
12. Would you rather live in the .... or the country?
13. If everyone used mass .... , traffic jams would disappear.

14. (down) There are more .... in a city than a small town.

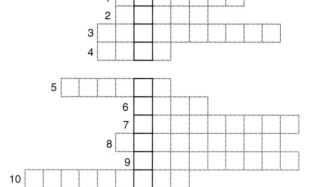

Puzzle B The words in this puzzle are from Lessons 25–26. Read the sentences below. Then complete the puzzle with the missing words.

1. Most art museums contain more .... than sculptures.
2. A painting of a person is a .... .

3. Do you prefer figurative or .... art?
4. The colors in that painting aren't dark. They're .... .
5. Do you like .... art, or do you prefer older works of art?

6. TV, films, and theater are different forms of .... .
7. Mozart and Beethoven are famous .... .
8. I read a .... of a film that said it was really good.
9. The guitar, violin, and saxophone are all .... .
10. I go to rock .... a few times a year.
11. I like all kinds of music including jazz and .... music.

12. (down) My favorite way of spending an evening is going .... .

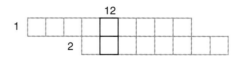
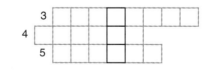
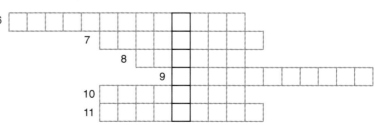

Activity C **Pair work** Look at these comic strips. Then discuss the questions below.

- Are either of these comic strips popular in your country?
- Which comic strip would people in your country find the funniest? the least funny? Why?
- What are the most popular comic strips in your country?

Activity D **Communication task** Work in groups of three or four. Look at Task 20 on page C-12. You're going to make up a story about a picture.

Review puzzles

Puzzle A   The words in this puzzle are from Lessons 27–28. Read the sentences below. Then complete the puzzle with the missing words.

1. A word that means "very old" is .... .
2. Stonehenge is built of .... .

3. Kiyomizu is a .... in Japan.
4. It's interesting to visit .... sights and buildings such as Kiyomizu and Teotihuacán.
5. Do you .... when you were twelve years old? Were you different then?

6. Two thousand years ago, Teotihuacán was the .... of a state of 10,000 people.
7. Some people believe that Stonehenge was an ancient temple and .... ground.
8. A .... has a lot of exhibits that tell you about the past.
9. When I was a child, I .... drink a lot of milk.

10. (down) History is about what happened ....

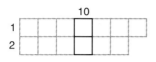
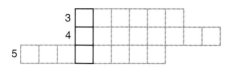
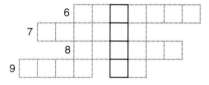

Puzzle B   The words in this puzzle are from Lessons 29–30. Read the sentences below. Then complete the puzzle with the missing words.

1. A .... is a funny drawing.
2. A word that means "very, very funny" is .... .
3. A .... strip is a row of funny drawings in a newspaper.
4. She laughed and .... when she told her friend about the funny thing that happened in class.
5. A .... is someone who performs in comedy shows.
6. Listen, I'm going to tell you a funny .... .

7. He never thinks anything is funny. He's got no .... of humor.
8. That comedian always makes me .... .
9. He always tells .... . He's very funny.
10. A .... is a funny person who performs in the circus.

11. (down) What's your favorite .... on TV?

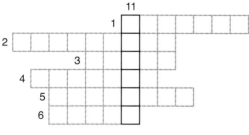
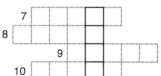

Communication tasks

Task 1 Ask your partner the questions in the survey below and check (✔) the answers. Use the adjectives in the box on the left to make statements about your partner's personality. Then your partner will ask you questions.

active/relaxed
casual/formal
shy/outgoing
organized/disorganized
neat/messy

1. When you take a walk, do you walk . . . ?
☐ fast   ☐ average speed   ☐ slow

2. When you go to a party, do you usually wear . . . ?
☐ casual clothes like jeans and a T-shirt
☐ more formal clothing (a dress or skirt for women, a jacket and tie for men)

3. In your free time, do you prefer to . . . ?
☐ read a book   ☐ go dancing

4. How often do you begin conversations with strangers?
☐ often   ☐ sometimes   ☐ never

5. What does your bedroom look like?
☐ The bed is unmade. Clothes are lying on the floor.
☐ The bed is made. Clothes are put away in the dresser or closet.

I think you're an active person because you walk fast. You're shy because . . .

Task 2 Join another group. Bring the menu you wrote in your first group and act out a restaurant scene. You are the waiter or waitress. The others in your group are the customers. Give your menu to the customers and give them some time to decide what to order. Answer their questions about the food on the menu and take their order. Remember to ask your customers what they want to drink.

You have just moved to a new town and want to make some friends. Look at the pictures of these people and listen to your partner tell you about them. Then choose one person you would like to be friends with. Explain your choice.

Scott Simmons

Debbie Malnick

Peter Ito

Now describe the three people below to your partner. Your partner will choose one person to be friends with. Ask your partner about his or her choice.

Pam Sawyer
age: 23
occupation: musician
hobbies: ballroom dancing, tennis, going to movies
motto: Take time to stop and smell the flowers.

Carlos Garcia
age: 25
occupation: teacher
hobbies: visiting museums, playing the violin, swimming
motto: If at first you don't succeed, try, try again.

Penny Lee
age: 34
occupation: designer
hobbies: hang gliding, bungee jumping, going to rock concerts
motto: There's an exception to every rule.

Here are descriptions of two of the jobs in Activity B1 on page 21. Describe the jobs to your group without mentioning the names of the jobs. Ask your group to guess which jobs you're talking about.

ANIMAL TRAINER

An animal trainer works on a movie set when animals are being used in a movie. It is the trainer's job to teach animals how to perform in front of the camera. Animal trainers work with all kinds of animals. They teach dogs to sit, bears to dance, and dolphins to jump.

GRIP

A grip sets up and moves the equipment on a movie set. He or she also helps with the lights and cameras. A grip is also in charge of renting any equipment that is needed on the movie set. He or she must know all of the equipment and what it's used for.

This person works on a movie set . . .

Look at these photos. Work together and try to guess what the products do. How do you think they work?

Each person in your group has a description of one of the items above. Take turns asking and answering questions about the products. Find out as much information as you can.

Picture One

It's a flashlight, an emergency flasher, and a lighter!

LITEMATE combines three useful lights in one unit. You can use it at home, in your car, or when you're camping. LITEMATE is perfect for emergencies. On one end of LITEMATE, there's a flashlight. On the other end, there's a red emergency light that flashes. At the bottom, there's a long lighter that comes apart from the rest of the unit. It's perfect for lighting candles or starting a campfire. Uses four batteries.

$29.95

Look at the photos below and decide what this recently married couple did on their vacation.

Now that you have decided on a story, find a pair of students who looked at the photos in Task 9. Find out the story behind their photos. Then tell them your story. What do the two vacations have in common? List at least three things.

Task 7   Work with your partner and look at this information about Ireland and Australia.

Republic of Ireland (Eire)

- Area: 70,000 sq km/27,000 sq mi
- Population: 3,500,000
- Population density: 50 people per sq km/130 per sq mi
- Average temperature: January 7°C/45°F
                                June 14°C/58°F
- Largest city: Dublin (1 million people)
- Highest mountain: Mt. Carrauntoohill (1,041 m/3,414 ft)
- Percentage of land that is wilderness: 5%
- Length of coastline: 1,448 km/900 mi
- Number of tourists who visit per year: 3,100,000

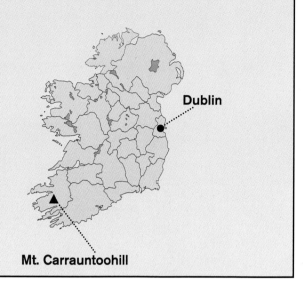

Australia

- Area: 7,700,000 sq km/3,000,000 sq mi
- Population: 18,000,000
- Population density: 2 people per sq km/6 per sq mi
- Average temperature: January 28°C/82°F
                                June 18°C/64°F
- Largest city: Sydney (3.6 million people)
- Highest mountain: Mt. Kosciusko (2,228 m/7,310 ft)
- Percentage of land that is wilderness: 14%
- Length of coastline: 25,760 km/16,010 mi
- Number of tourists who visit per year: 2,600,000

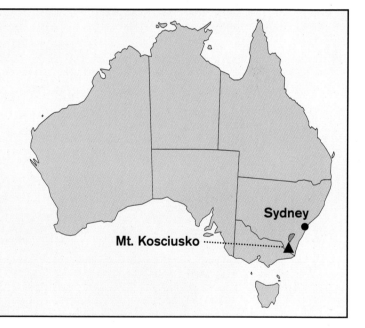

Join the rest of your group. They have information about Canada and New Zealand. Work together and answer the questions below.

1. Which country has the largest land mass? ....

2. Which country has the largest percentage of wilderness? ....

3. Which country has the highest population density? ....

4. Which is the warmest country? ....

5. Which country has the highest mountain? ....

6. Which two countries have cities of over 3 million people? ....

Now imagine you want to study English for a year in one of the four countries your group talked about. Decide which country you would like to study in and tell the group why.

Task 8   What environmental problems do the photos show? Describe the problems to your partner. Your partner will suggest some solutions.

garbage
bottles and cans
pollution
smog

The first picture shows . . .
In the second picture, . . .

Task 9   Look at the photos below and decide what this recently married couple did on their vacation.

Now that you have decided on a story, find a pair of students who looked at the photos in Task 6. Tell them the story behind your photos. Then listen to their story. What do the two vacations have in common? List at least three things.

Task 10 Look at these photos. Work together and try to guess what the products do. How do you think they work?

Each person in your group has a description of one of the items above. Take turns asking and answering questions about the products. Find out as much information as you can.

Picture Two

Sparkling Sip™ Straw

You'll have cleaner drinking water instantly!

The portable Sparkling Sip™ straw can go with you anywhere. It removes chlorine, and bad tastes and smells from drinking water. The Sparkling Sip™ straw uses two filters to clean your drinking water.

One filter removes up to 95% of the chlorine present in drinking water. The other filter removes bad tastes and smells. Includes replacement filters and a carrying case.

$12.95

Task 11 Here are descriptions of two of the jobs in Activity B1 on page 21. Describe the jobs to your group without mentioning the names of the jobs. Ask your group to guess which jobs you're talking about.

CAMERAPERSON

A cameraperson looks through the lens of a camera and actually films the movie. He or she moves the camera up and down or left and right to keep the actors in the movie scene. The cameraperson often sits above the actors in a seat attached to the camera to film a scene.

MAKEUP ARTIST

A makeup artist is always on the movie set. Sometimes an artist applies makeup, like lipstick, to bring out an actor's natural color under the lights on the set. Other times the makeup artist has to turn the actor into a different character, such as a monster or a clown.

This person looks through the lens of a camera . . .

Task 12   First, answer your partner's questions. Then ask your partner the questions in the survey below and check (✔) the answers. Use the adjectives in the box on the left to make statements about your partner's personality.

1. How often do you talk to friends on the telephone?
   ☐ all the time   ☐ quite often   ☐ not very often

2. In your free time, do you prefer to . . . ?
   ☐ play sports   ☐ watch a movie

active/relaxed
casual/formal
shy/outgoing
organized/disorganized
neat/messy

3. When you shop, do you usually . . . ?
   ☐ make a list of what you need before you go out
   ☐ buy whatever looks good

4. When you use a textbook to study English, do you . . . ?
   ☐ scribble words and answers anywhere on the page
   ☐ write carefully on the lines provided

5. What kind of party do you prefer?
   ☐ A loud, crowded party that has music and dancing.
   ☐ A small dinner party.

I think you're outgoing because you talk to friends on the phone all the time. You're active because . . .

Task 13   A person from another group will join the two of you. Act out a restaurant scene. The new person will give you a menu. He or she is the waiter. You are customers. You are foreign visitors, not local residents. Look at the menu and ask the waiter or waitress to explain some of the items on the menu. Then decide what to order.

Task 14 Your partner has just moved to a new town and wants to make some friends. Describe each of these people to your partner. Your partner will choose one person to be friends with. Ask your partner about his or her choice.

Scott Simmons
age: 32
occupation: lawyer
hobbies: reading, going to concerts, cooking
motto: Actions speak louder than words.

Debbie Malnick
age: 26
occupation: student
hobbies: painting, dancing, Rollerblading
motto: Look before you leap.

Peter Ito
age: 26
occupation: computer programmer
hobbies: sailing, rock climbing, traveling
motto: Never walk when you can run.

Now *you* have just moved to a new town and want to make some friends. Your partner tells you about the three people below. Look at the pictures and listen to your partner tell you about each person. Then choose one person you would like to be friends with. Explain your choice.

Pam Sawyer

Carlos Garcia

Penny Lee

Task 15 Here are descriptions of two of the jobs in Activity B1 on page 21. Describe the jobs to your group without mentioning the names of the jobs. Ask your group to guess which jobs you're talking about.

STUNTPERSON

A stuntperson takes an actor's place when a scene in a movie is too dangerous. Jumping off buildings and driving cars very fast are just some of the things that a stuntperson does. This is the most dangerous job in film production and safety classes are required.

FILM EDITOR

A film editor begins work after the movie has been filmed. He or she looks at the film and decides which parts of the movie to cut because they are too long or boring. The film editor uses a special machine to cut out pieces of film and put other pieces together, a process called splicing film.

This person takes an actor's place when . . .

Task 16 Look at these photos. Work together and try to guess what the products do. How do you think they work?

Each person in your group has a description of one of the items above. Take turns asking and answering questions about the products. Find out as much information as you can.

Picture Three

HANG UPS™ Heavy Duty Inversion Table

Fight stress and back pain with Hang Ups™ Heavy Duty Inversion Table. Strap yourself into the ankle holders and move into a comfortable position. An adjustable strap stops the table at any position.

Hang Ups™ Heavy Duty Inversion Table comes with an instructional video and a 90-page book, *Better Back, Better Body.* Holds up to 300 pounds.

$399.95

Task 17 Your partner is going to describe some environmental problems to you. Look at the photos below and suggest some solutions to the problems.

recycle
public transportation

One solution to this problem is . . .
It's a good idea to . . .

Task 18   Work with your partner and study this information about Canada and New Zealand.

Canada

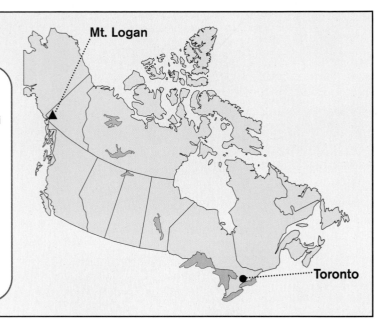

- Area: 10,000,000 sq km/4,000,000 sq mi
- Population: 29,000,000
- Population density: 3 people per sq km/8 per sq mi
- Average temperature: January -9°C/16°F
  June 12°C/54°F
- Largest city: Toronto (3.9 million people)
- Highest mountain: Mt. Logan (5,959 m/19,551 ft)
- Percentage of land that is wilderness: 35%
- Length of coastline: 243,791 km/151,492 mi
- Number of tourists who visit per year: 36,000,000
- Canada has two official languages: English (20,000,000 speakers) and French (8,000,000 speakers)

New Zealand

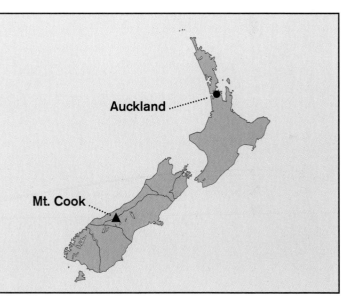

- Area: 270,000 sq km/100,000 sq mi
- Population: 3,500,000
- Population density: 13 people per sq km/34 per sq mi
- Average temperature: January 18°C/64°F
  June 8°C/46°F
- Largest city: Auckland (900,000 people)
- Highest mountain: Mt. Cook (3,764 m/12,349 ft)
- Percentage of land that is wilderness: 38%
- Length of coastline: 15,134 km/9,406 mi
- Number of tourists who visit per year: 1,100,000

Join the rest of your group. They have information about Ireland and Australia. Work together and answer the questions below.

1. Which country has the largest land mass? ....

2. Which country has the largest percentage of wilderness? ....

3. Which country has the highest population density? ....

4. Which is the warmest country? ....

5. Which country has the highest mountain? ....

6. Which two countries have cities of over 3 million people? ....

Now imagine you want to study English for a year in one of the four countries your group talked about. Decide which country you would like to study in and tell the group why.

Ask your partner about the activities in the photos and write his or her answers below. If your partner doesn't know what an activity is, try to explain it without showing him or her the photo. Then answer your partner's questions.

Have you ever been bungee jumping? ....

If so, what was it like? ....

....

If not, would you like to try it? Why or why not?

....

....

Have you ever been hang gliding? ....

If so, what was it like? ....

....

If not, would you like to try it? Why or why not?

....

....

Task 20 Think of a funny story to explain the photo below. Answer these questions.
- Who is the person in the photo?
- What has just happened?
- What's going to happen next?

Compare your story with another group. How are your stories alike? In what ways are they different?

Task 21 Imagine that the events pictured below happened to you a long time ago. The scenes show the beginning, middle, and end of a story. With your partner, figure out what happened in between. Then take on the role of one of the people in the pictures and "reminisce" with your partner about what happened.

> *Do you remember the time we went . . . ?*
> *I'll never forget how you . . .*
>
> *Do you remember what we did after that?*
> *Yeah, we . . .*

scene 1

scene 2

scene 3

After you have prepared your story, form a pair with another student, who has prepared a story about the pictures in Task 32. Tell your story to your new partner as if you are one of the characters. Then listen to your new partner's story.

> *I'll never forget the time I . . .*
> *Then you'll never guess what happened . . .*
>
> *The next thing that happened was . . .*
> *We felt really . . . when . . .*

Task 22 Try to understand and memorize the main points of these jokes. Then take turns telling them to your group.

> **Doctor:** You need glasses.
> **Woman:** But I'm already wearing glasses.
> **Doctor:** In that case, *I* need glasses.

> **Man:** What's the secret to a long, happy marriage?
> **Woman:** Well, my husband and I go out for a fancy dinner every week.
> **Man:** That's wonderful! Where do you go?
> **Woman:** I go to my favorite Italian restaurant – I don't know where my husband goes.

Now discuss these questions.
- Which jokes did you think were funny? Which jokes didn't you like?
- Do you know any other jokes? Tell one to your group.

Task 23

You want to visit one of the cities pictured below, but need to find out more information about each one before making a choice.

San Francisco, California, U.S.A.

Rio de Janeiro, Brazil

Ask your partner questions about:
- the weather
- popular foods
- popular tourist sights
- the average price of a hotel room
- the average price of dinner for two

After you find out about the cities, choose the one you would most like to visit.

> What's the weather like in . . . ?   How much does a hotel room cost in . . . ?

Now it's your partner's turn. He or she is going to choose between one of the cities described below. Answer your partner's questions using the information below. Then ask your partner to decide on a city to visit. Find out about his or her choice.

Seoul, Korea

Average temperature:	January -1°C/30°F
	June 27°C/81°F
Average cost of a hotel room:	$170 a night
Average cost of a dinner for two:	$50

Food specialties

Pulgogi: beef marinated with soy sauce and other spices

Kimch'i: a spicy vegetable dish made of cabbage

Tourist attractions

Secret Garden: part of a royal palace; famous for its beautiful scenery

Namdaemun Market: a great place to shop for bargains

Mt. Puk'ansan: a national park with Buddhist temples and interesting hiking paths

Venice, Italy

Average temperature:	January 4°C/40°F
	June 27°C/81°F
Average cost of a hotel room:	$100 a night
Average cost of a dinner for two:	$60

Food specialties

Fegato alla Veneziana: calf's liver served on a bed of onions

Polenta: grilled cornmeal served with sauce

Tourist attractions

Basilica di San Marco: a cathedral with beautiful artwork, marble, and carvings

Rialto Quarter: the oldest and busiest part of the city – a great place to shop

Lagoon Islands: once the home of fishermen and hunters, these nearby islands attract many tourists

> Which city would you like to visit?   Why did you choose . . . ?

Task 24

Take turns. Think of a famous person you admire. The others in your group will ask you *yes/no* questions about this person. Answer the questions, but remember you can only respond by saying "yes" or "no." After a few minutes, the others in your group will try to guess the person you are thinking about. Tell the group if their guess is correct. Then say why you admire the famous person you chose.

Now someone else in your group should think of a famous person. Ask *yes/no* questions and try to guess who the person is.

> Is this person male?   Is he/she still alive?   Does he/she act in the movies?

Task 25

Are you a reliable witness? Work with a partner and discuss these questions about the photo on page 50. Use your memory to answer the questions. Don't look back at page 50.
- What was the weather like that day?
- How many cars were there? Where were they?
- How many people were there?
- How many people were standing on the bench?
- How many people were standing on the sidewalk?
- How many people's faces could you see?
- How many people were wearing hats?
- What was the woman on the left holding?
- Where was the woman on the right standing? What was she holding?
- Where exactly was the man standing? What was he wearing?

Now don't look back at page 50, but join another pair. Compare your answers to the questions.

Task 26

Try to understand and memorize the main points of these jokes. Then take turns telling them to your group.

> **Teacher:** If you had $5, and you asked your dad for $5, how much would you have?
> **Student:** Um . . . $5.
> **Teacher:** You don't know your math!
> **Student:** You don't know my dad!

> Two goats are busy eating garbage. One goat finds a roll of old film and chews it up.
> **Goat 1:** Did you enjoy the film?
> **Goat 2:** Actually, I preferred the book.

Now discuss these questions.
- Which jokes did you think were funny? Which jokes didn't you like?
- Do you know any other jokes? Tell one to your group.

Task 27　Take turns. Choose the painting you like best and describe it to your partner in terms of color, style, and mood. Have your partner guess which painting you are describing.

color	style	mood
bright/subtle	abstract/figurative	happy/sad
varied/similar	classic/modern	peaceful/tense
vibrant/dull		romantic/unromantic

Now join another pair and discuss these questions.
- Which couple do you think has the best relationship? Why?
- Which couple do you think has the worst relationship? Why?

Task 28　Take turns. Think of a famous person you admire. The others in your group will ask you *yes/no* questions about this person. Answer the questions, but remember you can only respond by saying "yes" or "no." After a few minutes, the others in your group will try to guess the person you are thinking about. Tell the group if their guess is correct. Then say why you admire the famous person you chose.

Now someone else in your group should think of a famous person. Ask *yes/no* questions and try to guess who the person is.

Is this person male?　Is he/she still alive?　Does he/she act in the movies?

Task 29

First, answer your partner's questions. Then ask your partner about the activities in the photos. Write his or her answers below. If your partner doesn't know what an activity is, try to explain it without showing him or her the photo.

Have you ever been Rollerblading?....................

If so, what was it like?...................................

....

If not, would you like to try it? Why or why not?

....

....

Have you ever been skydiving?.........................

If so, what was it like?...................................

....

If not, would you like to try it? Why or why not?

....

....

Task 30

Try to understand and memorize the main points of these jokes. Then take turns telling them to your group.

Teacher: If I had three oranges in one hand and four oranges in the other, what would I have?
Student: Very big hands!

Patient: How can I live to be 100?
Doctor: Give up cookies, cake, and ice cream. Stop eating red meat and bread – and no soft drinks.
Patient: And if I do all of that, will I live to be 100?
Doctor: Maybe not, but it will certainly seem like it!

Now discuss these questions.
• Which jokes did you think were funny? Which jokes didn't you like?
• Do you know any other jokes? Tell one to your group.

Your partner is going to visit one of the cities described below, but needs more information before making a choice. Answer your partner's questions using the information below. Then ask your partner to decide on a city to visit. Find out about his or her choice.

San Francisco, California, U.S.A.

Average temperature:	January 16°C/60°F
	June 24°C/75°F
Average cost of a hotel room:	$90 a night
Average cost of a dinner for two:	$60

Food specialties
Sourdough bread: a tasty bread made with sourdough

California roll: avocado, carrot, cucumber, and rice wrapped in seaweed

Tourist attractions
Golden Gate Park: sight of a Japanese Tea Garden

Chinatown: interesting architecture and good places to eat

Ghirardelli Square: a modern shopping mall with a great view of the water

Rio de Janeiro, Brazil

Average temperature:	January 27°C/81°F
	June 24°C/75°F
Average cost of a hotel room:	$100 a night
Average cost of a dinner for two:	$40

Food specialties
Feijoada: a stew made of meat and black beans

Farofa: flour cooked in butter with chopped olives, bacon, and hard-boiled eggs

Tourist attractions
Copacabana Beach: a beautiful beach near hotels and restaurants

National Park of Tijuca: one of the largest city parks in the world with a garden and places to hike

Native American Museum: artifacts such as Native American clothing, jewelry, and tools

> *Which city would you like to visit?*   *Why did you choose . . . ?*

Now it's your turn. You want to visit one of these cities.

Seoul, Korea

Venice, Italy

Ask your partner questions about:
- the weather
- popular foods
- popular tourist sights
- the average price of a hotel room
- the average price of dinner for two

After you find out more about the cities, choose the one you would most like to visit.

> *What's the weather like in . . . ?*   *How much does a hotel room cost in . . . ?*

Task 32

Imagine that the events pictured below happened to you a long time ago. The scenes show the beginning, middle, and end of a story. With your partner, figure out what happened in between. Then take on the role of one of the people in the pictures and "reminisce" with your partner about what happened.

> Do you remember the time we went . . . ?
> I'll never forget how you . . .

> Do you remember what we did after that?
> Yeah, we . . .

scene 1

scene 2

scene 3

After you have prepared your story, form a pair with another student, who has prepared a story about the pictures in Task 21. Tell your story to your new partner as if you are one of the characters. Then listen to your new partner's story.

> I'll never forget the time I . . .
> Then you'll never guess what happened . . .

> The next thing that happened was . . .
> We felt really . . . when . . .

Task 33

Take turns. Think of a famous person you admire. The others in your group will ask you *yes/no* questions about this person. Answer the questions, but remember you can only respond by saying "yes" or "no." After a few minutes, the others in your group will try to guess the person you are thinking about. Tell the group if their guess is correct. Then say why you admire the famous person you chose.

Now someone else in your group should think of a famous person. Ask *yes/no* questions and try to guess who the person is.

> Is this person male?   Is he/she still alive?   Does he/she act in the movies?

Task 34   To find out your score to the sports quiz on page 43:
1. Add up all of the numbers in the *Participate in* column of the quiz.
2. Add up the numbers in the *Watch* column of the quiz.
3. Look at the chart below to find out what your score means.

Participating in sports

less than 25: You aren't an active person. You avoid playing sports whenever possible.

26–50: You're somewhat active, but not what we'd call a sports nut.

51–150: You're an active person, and you like playing a lot of different sports.

151–250: You're a sports nut. You've tried a lot of different sports and still spend a lot of time exercising.

over 250: Wow! You must be a professional athlete! (Or maybe you added your numbers up wrong!)

Watching sports

less than 10: You *really* hate watching sports.

11–50: You like sports, but you don't watch them that often.

51–100: You're a sports fan. You really enjoy watching different sports.

101–150: You're a sports nut. Sports are a very important part of your life.

over 150: Hmm, this is a very high score. Do you think sports may be taking over your life? Do you have time for anything else?

Answers   **Page 57 The answers below follow the order of the art on page 56 (clockwise from top right).**

Orpheus and Eurydice by Nicolas Poussin (circa 1659)

The Two Fridas by Frida Kahlo (1939)

Composition with Grey, Red, Yellow, and Blue by Piet Mondrian (1920)

Galloping Horse by Xu Beihong (circa 1950)

Red Poppy by Georgia O'Keeffe (1927)

Male Torso by Fernando Botero (1992)

Acknowledgments

Text Credits

27 Adapted from SCHOLASTIC UPDATE, April 16, 1993.
Copyright © 1993 by Scholastic Inc. Reprinted by permission.

53 © 1995 The Economist Newspaper Group, Inc.
Reprinted with permission. Further reproduction prohibited.

Illustrations

Paulette Bogan 69
David Gothard 11, 12, 19, 60
Randy Jones 4, 40, 65, C-13, C-19
Wally Neibart 30, 38

Photographic Credits

The author and publisher are grateful for permission to reproduce the following photographs.

Cover photos: (background) © Darryl Torckler/Tony Stone Images; *(top row: left)* © Mark Scott/
FPG International; *(right)* © Michael Keller/FPG International; *(middle row: both)* © Ron Chapple/
FPG International; *(bottom row: left)* © Ed Taylor Studio/FPG International; *(right)* © Ken Fisher/
Tony Stone Images

2 *(top row)* © Tom Campbell/FPG International; © The Stock Market/Gabe Palmer, 1989;
(bottom row) © Jean-Marc Truchet/Tony Stone Images; © Art Tilley/FPG International

5 *(clockwise from top left)* © Comstock, Inc.; © Innervisions, 1995; © Stewart Cohen/
Tony Stone Images

7 *(top)* © The Stock Market/Randy Duchaine, 1986; *(bottom)* © The Stock Market/
David Pollack, 1993

8 *(clockwise from top left)* © Steven Needham/Envision; © Guy Powers/Envision; © Eric Futran/
Gamma Liaison; © Michael Keller/FPG International

13 *(clockwise from top left)* © The Stock Market/Ronnie Kaufman, 1993; © Dick Luria/
FPG International; © The Stock Market/Paul Barton, 1993

14 *(clockwise: top left)* Photofest; *(right and bottom left)* The Kobal Collection

16 *(left to right: 1, 2, 4, 5)* © Ron Chapple/FPG International; *(3)* © L.O.L. Inc./
FPG International; *(6)* © Stephen Simpson/FPG International

18 *(left to right: 1, 4)* © Innervisions, 1995; *(2, 3)* © Comstock, Inc.

20 © Innervisions, 1995

21 *(top row)* © Randy Taylor/Gamma Liaison; © François Darmigny/Gamma Liaison;
(middle row) © Comstock, Inc./Torrey D. Lepp; The Kobal Collection; *(bottom row)*
© Innervisions, 1995; © Jean Marc Giboux/Gamma Liaison

22 *(microwave oven)* © Comstock, Inc./Bob Pizaro; *(photocopier, answering machine, clock radio)*
© Innervisions, 1995; *(mouse)* © The Stock Market/Peter Steiner, 1991; *(camcorder)*
© The Stock Market/Roy Schneider; *(remote control, fax machine)* © SuperStock

24 *(Pencorder)* Courtesy of Machina, Inc.; *(Safe-T-Man)* Courtesy of The Safety Zone;
(TV Remote Control Locator) Courtesy of VITRA Products Inc.

25 *(top and middle)* © Innervisions, 1995; *(bottom)* © John Brooks/Gamma Liaison

26 *(left to right)* © Gary Buss/FPG International; © The Stock Market/Ken Straiton, 1988;
© Jean Higgins/Envision

27 *(left)* © Daniel J. Cox/Gamma Liaison; *(right)* © David Bartruff/FPG International

29 *(top: all)* © Innervisions, 1995; *(bottom: left to right)* © Glen Allison/Tony Stone Images;
© The Stock Market/Chris Rogers; © The Stock Market/Mug Shots, 1993

31 *(top row)* © The Stock Market/Chris McLaughlin, 1991; © S. Kanno/FPG International;
(bottom row) © Martin Barraud/Tony Stone Images; © Eugen Gebhardt/FPG International

32 *(left to right)* © The Stock Market/Roy Morsch; © The Stock Market/Gabe Palmer, 1992;
© SuperStock

33 *(top row)* © FPG International; © Chan Bush/FPG International; *(middle row)*
© The Stock Market/Thomas Braise, 1982; © The Stock Market/Alan Schein; *(bottom row)*
© The Stock Market/Albano Guatti, 1985; © The Stock Market/Tom Martin, 1980

34 *(clockwise from top)* Bowman/Leo de Wys, Inc.; © John Lamb/Tony Stone Images;
© Randy Wells/Tony Stone Images

35 *(left to right)* © John Lamb/Tony Stone Images; © Val Corbett/Tony Stone Images;
© The Stock Market/Markova, 1989

39 *(clockwise from left)* © The Stock Market/Don Mason, 1994; © Dick Luria/FPG International;
© The Stock Market/Ted Mahieu, 1989; © Comstock, Inc./Jack Elness

42 *(clockwise from top left)* © The Stock Market/Lewis Portnoy, 1984; © Eugen Gebhardt/
FPG International; © The Stock Market/Aaron Chang, 1994

44 © Innervisions, 1995

46 *(clockwise from top)* © The Stock Market/Milt Putnam, 1990; © Stephen Rose/
Gamma Liaison; © AP/Wide World Photos; © John Darling/Tony Stone Images

50 Hulton Getty

52 *(top row)* © Timothy Shonnard/Tony Stone Images; © Comstock, Inc./Art Gingert;
(bottom row) © J.B. Marshall/Envision; © Paul Chesley/Tony Stone Images

56 *(clockwise from top right)* Nicolas Poussin, *Orpheus and Eurydice,* c. 1659. Louvre.
Erich Lessing/Art Resource, NY; Frida Kahlo, *The Two Fridas,* 1939. Museo Nacional de
Arte Moderno, Mexico City, D.F., Mexico. Schalkwijk/Art Resource, NY; Piet Mondrian,
Composition with Grey, Red, Yellow, and Blue, 1920. Tate Gallery, London, GB. © Mondrian
Estate/Holtzman Trust. Tate Gallery, London/Art Resource, NY; Xu Beihong, *Galloping Horse,*
c. 1950. Christie's London/SuperStock; Georgia O'Keeffe, *Red Poppy,* 1927. © 1997 The Georgia
O'Keeffe Foundation/Artists Rights Society (ARS), New York. Art Resource, NY; Fernando Botero,
Male Torso, 1992. © J.C. Francolon/Gamma Liaison

57 *(left to right)* © Wenzel Fischer/FPG International; © The Stock Market/Pete Saloutos, 1988;
Giraudon/Art Resource, NY; © Innervisions, 1996; © Biondo Productions/Gamma Liaison;
© Simon Daniel/Gamma Liaison

58 *(top row)* © The Stock Market/G&G Design, 1989; Photofest; *(bottom row)* Steve Rapport/
© London Features Int'l. USA Ltd.; © Charlie Westerman/Gamma Liaison

59 Photofest

62 *(both)* © Innervisions, 1996

64 *(left to right)* © Shinichi Kanno/FPG International; © The Stock Market/Tibor Bognár;
© Telegraph Colour Library/FPG International

66 *(top row)* The Kobal Collection; Photofest; *(bottom row: both)* The Kobal Collection

67 *(left to right: 1, 2, 4)* Photofest; *(3)* The Kobal Collection

C-3 *(left and middle)* © Ron Chapple/FPG International; *(right)* © L.O.L. Inc./FPG International

C-4, C-7, C-10 *(Litemate)* Courtesy of Polyflame Concepts U.S.A. Inc.;
(Sparkling Sip™ Straw) Courtesy of Hydro Life, Incorporated;
(Hang Ups™ Heavy Duty Inversion Table) Courtesy of STL International, Inc.

C-4 *(bottom row: all)* © The Stock Market/R.B. Studio, 1994

C-6 *(top row)* © Kevin Schafer/Tony Stone Images; Foulon/Leo de Wys, Inc.; *(bottom row: all)*
© The Stock Market/R.B. Studio, 1994

C-9 *(left and middle)* © Ron Chapple/FPG International; *(right)* © Stephen Simpson/
FPG International

C-10 *(bottom row)* © The Stock Market/Craig Hammell, 1992; © The Stock Market/
B. Harrington III, 1994

C-12 *(top)* © Frederick McKinney/FPG International; *(middle)* SuperStock;
(bottom) FPG International

C-14 *(left)* © The Stock Market/Wes Thompson, 1987; *(right)* © Will & Deni McIntyre/
Tony Stone Images

C-16 *(middle)* Amedeo Modigliani, *Bride and Groom (The Couple).* Museum of Modern Art, NY/
Lerner Collection/SuperStock; *(right)* Jan Van Eyck, *The Arnolfini Marriage.* National Gallery,
London/SuperStock

C-17 © Scott Markewitz/FPG International; © The Stock Market/Tom Sanders, 1993

C-18 Korean National Tourism Organization; © Chad Ehlers/Tony Stone Images

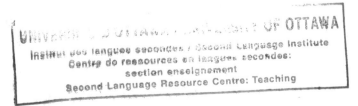